CODE, COMMUNITY, MINISTRY

SELECTED STUDIES FOR THE PARISH MINISTER
INTRODUCING THE REVISED CODE OF CANON LAW

EDITED BY JAMES H. PROVOST

Canon Law Society of America
Washington, DC 20064

The materials that appear in this book (except those for which reprint permission must be obtained from the primary sources) may be freely reproduced for educational/training activities. There is no requirement to obtain special permission for such uses. We do ask, however, that the following statement appear on all reproductions:

This permission statement is limited to the reproduction of materials for educational/training events. *Systematic or large-scale reproduction or distribution — or inclusion of items in publications for sale — may be done only with prior written permission.*

Published by
Canon Law Society of America
Catholic University of America
Washington, DC 20064
Phone: (202) 269-3491

CONTENTS

INTRODUCTION

A growing discovery in the post-Vatican II Church has been the pastoral potential to be found in the Church's law. Church law is broader than a set of canons or detailed prescriptions. It reflects the fundamental communion of the Church and is directed toward fostering the mission of all the people of God.

The promulgation of the revised Code of Canon Law by Pope John Paul II on January 25, 1983 marks another step in this discovery. In his Apostolic Constitution introducing the new Code, John Paul II repeated the expectations of Popes John XXIII and Paul VI that the revised Code would be an important element in implementing the spirit and teachings of the Second Vatican Council. The revised Code, he pointed out, is distinguished by its spirit of collegiality. It recognizes that we are saved by faith, not law. The Code is meant to be an instrument to promote the communion of the Church at its various levels and in its many members.

Law texts tend to be technical and dry. It takes an added effort at times to appreciate their pastoral significance, or to explore the opportunities a revised Code presents the Church to continue the work of renewal based in the teachings of Vatican II. To help in this effort, a series of short studies was put together for workshops conducted by the Canon Law Society of America in the summer of 1982 for diocesan administrators. These study papers address the pastoral implications and opportunities of the revised Code, and attempt to explain the Code's significance for various aspects of pastoral ministry.

Now the C.L.S.A. is pleased to make these studies available to a wider audience. To the original collection has been added an initial study to set the framework for understanding Church law today. The Jesuit scholar and Council expert John Courtney Murray penned this work in 1966, not long before he died. Law in the Church today must be placed in the perspective he set, fresh from the Council and conscious of the American Catholic experience. Rather than a branch of moral theology, Church law pertains to the broader context of Church order. Murray's work addresses that context, and was distributed in advance to the participants at the 1982 C.L.S.A. workshops.

The remainder of the papers are the work of Canon Law Society of America members. They are designed not so much as technical commentaries on the revised Code—another C.L.S.A. project is attending to that need. Rather, these are efforts to place various aspects of the law into a pastoral setting which may help those interested in the daily life of the Church appreciate the opportunities and possibilities contained in this revised Code. Although they were drafted when only the proposed text (or "schema") was available, the studies have been edited to conform to the provisions of the promulgated Code. Canon numbers cited have been corrected in keeping with those in the final text.

A special word of appreciation is expressed to Bertram F. Griffin, J.C.D., Archdiocese of Portland-in-Oregon, who contributed the bulk of these studies. Appreciation is also expressed to the other C.L.S.A. members who contributed studies: John A. Alesandro, J.C.D., Diocese of Rockville Centre, New York; James A. Coriden, J.C.D., Washington Theological Union; Richard G. Cunningham, J.C.D., Archdiocese of Boston; Thomas J. Green, J.C.D., Catholic University of America; Richard A. Hill, S.J., J.C.D., Jesuit School of Theology at Berkeley, California; Kenneth E. Lasch, J.C.D., Diocese of Paterson, New Jersey; James H. Provost, J.C.D., Catholic University of America; and Royce R. Thomas, J.C.L., Diocese of Little Rock, Arkansas. Acknowledgement is made to *America* magazine for permission to reprint the article by John Courtney Murray, and to N.C. News Service for the use of their English translation of John Paul II's Apostolic Constitution, "Sacrae disciplinae leges."

FREEDOM, AUTHORITY, COMMUNITY

Some people today speak of a "crisis of authority" in the Church, others speak of a "crisis of freedom." For my own part, I should prefer to speak of a "crisis of community." The reasons for this description of the situation will appear, I hope, in what follows.

Vatican Council II did not create the crisis; its roots are deep in the past. But the Council brought the crisis into the open. In the first place, the Declaration on Religious Freedom (*Dignitatis humanae*) said in effect, that in political society the human person is to live his relation with God, or even with his private idol, in freedom—within a zone of freedom juridically guaranteed against invasion by any form of coercion. This proposition, the Council added, is the product of a biblical insight though centuries of secular and religious experience were needed in order to bring it to explicit conceptualization.

In the second place, the Constitution on the Church in the Modern World (*Gaudium et spes*) affirmed, in effect, that the relation of the Church to the world and of the world to the Church is to be lived in freedom. Freedom, Paul VI said in his momentous address to statesmen on Dec. 8, 1965, is all that the Church asks of the political world—freedom for its apostolic ministry, freedom for the Christian life, freedom for spiritual and peaceful entrance into the political world, there to make moral judgments when political affairs raise moral issues. In turn, the constitution generously acknowledged that the world too has its rightful freedom to live its own life—or rather, its many lives: political, economic, social, cultural, scientific—in accordance with autonomous dynamisms and structures. These respective claims of freedom, the Council implied, are likewise rooted in a biblical insight—that the Church is of God, and so too, though in a different way, is the world.

Having laid down these propositions bearing on freedom, the Council inevitably raised the next question, concerning freedom in the Church. Is not the Christian life within the Christian community to be lived in freedom? Even the essential Christian experience of obedience to the authority of the Church—is it not somehow to be an experience of Christian freedom in the evangelical sense? This is the question, not directly touched by the Council, which now commands serious theological consideration in the light of the doctrine of the Council and of its spirit—indeed, in the light of the Council itself as a splendid "event of freedom" in the ongoing life of the Church.

1

I. FREEDOM AND AUTHORITY

A. *Classical Conception*

From a historical point of view, the need for new reflection on the relation between authority and freedom in the Church derives from the fact that presently this relation exhibits an imbalance. In order to grasp this fact, it will be sufficient for the moment to go back only as far as Leo XIII and to consider three aspects of his thought.

First, there is his retrospective reading of history, visible, for instance, in the famous "Once upon a time" paragraph (*Fuit aliquando tempus*) in *Immortale Dei*. Once upon a time there was a Golden Age, the medieval period. It was the age of Christian unity, of the alliance of the Two Powers, of the obedience of both princes and peoples to the authority of the Church. Then came the Reformation. Essentially it was a revolt against the authority of the Church, and in reaction to it the Church laid heavy, almost exclusive emphasis, on its own authority. Later, by a sequence that was not only historical but also logical, there came the Revolution. It was essentially a revolt against the authority of God Himself, launched by the revolutionary slogan: "No one stands above man" (*homini antistare nemimem*). Again in polemic reaction, the Church rallied to the defense of the sovereignty of God, of the "rights of God," of the doctrine that there is no true freedom except under the law of God.

Both of these reactions were historically inevitable and doctrinally justifiable. The Church fashions its doctrine under the signs of the times, and the Reformation and the Revolution were then the signs of the times. But the doctrine formed under them could not but exhibit a certain hypertrophy of the principle of authority, and a corresponding atrophy of the principle of freedom.

In the second place, there is Leo XIII's conception of the political relationship between ruler and ruled in civil society. It is a simple vertical relationship within which the ruled are merely subjects, whose single duty is obedience to authority. Only in the most inchoative fashion does one find in Leo the notion of the "citizen," who is equipped with political and civil rights and protected in their exercise. His emphasis falls on political authority, which is invested with a certain majesty as being from God, and which is to be exercised in paternal fashion in imitation of the divine sovereignty. In turn, the submission of the subject is to exhibit a certain filial quality. Moreover, society itself is to be built, as it were, from the top down. The "prince" is the primary bearer and agent of the social process. *Qualis rex, talis grex.* The ruler is to be the tutor and guardian of virtue in the body politic; the whole of the common good is committed to his charge. The people are simply the object of rule. Leo XIII's political doctrine was plainly authoritarian. It was fashioned under the political signs of the times — the laicist conception of the state and the Jacobin conception of the sovereignty of the people. In that moment in the history of continental Europe, Leo could not assume the patronage of political freedom.

2

In the third place, there is Leo XIII's ecclesiology, as summed up, for instance, in the encyclical *Satis Cognitum* (1896) in which he says: "We have faithfully depicted the image and figure *(imaginem atque formam)* of the Church as divinely established." The encyclical is, in effect, a lengthy, profound, magisterial commentary on the Vatican I constitution *Pastor Aeternus*, which was the splendid sign of the theological times. The portrait of the Church that emerges is really a portrait of the role of the apostolic office, and in particular the Petrine office, in the Church. In consequence, the ecclesial relationship — to call it such, on the analogy of the political relationship — is the simple vertical relationship between ruler and ruled. The function of the faithful appears simply as obedience to the doctrinal and jurisdictional authority of the Church.

It was within these perspectives that the classical doctrine on the relation of freedom and authority in the Church was fashioned. Those who hold office make the decisions, doctrinal and pastoral. The faithful in the ranks submit to the decisions and execute the orders. The concept of obedience is likewise simple. To obey is to do the will of the superior; that is the essence of obedience. And the perfection of obedience is to make the will of the superior one's own will. In both instances the motive is the vision of God in the superior, who is the mediator of the divine will and the agent of divine providence in regard of his subjects, in such wise that union with his will means union with the will of God. The further motive, to be adduced when obedience means self-sacrifice, is the vision of Christ, who made Himself obedient even unto death.

B. *New Signs of the Times*

The trouble is that this classical concept of the ecclesial relationship is today experienced as being true indeed, but not the whole truth — as being good indeed, but not good enough to meet the needs of the moment. The signs of the times are new. The age of anti-Reform polemic has gone over into the age of ecumenism. The will of the Church to break with the world of Revolution has given way to a new will to effect that "compenetration" between the Church of today and the world of today of which *Gaudium et spes* has spoken. The perspectives in which history is now viewed open out not from a supposed Golden Age in the past (whose luster is now seen to be dulled with the tarnish of much immaturity), but from the present moment. They are set not by nostalgia for the past, visible even in Leo XIII's *Satis Cognitum*, but by the solid doctrine of the eschatological character of the Christian existence, which requires it to look resolutely to the future — to the coming-to-be of the Kingdom.

New signs of the times have become visible and were fully recognized at Vatican Council II. The first is man's growing consciousness of his dignity as a person, which requires that he act on his own responsibility and therefore in freedom. The second is man's growing consciousness of community, of that being with the others and for the others which is revealed, for instance, in the phenomenon of "socialization" in the sense of *Mater et Magistra*. The Church in Council assembled clearly assumed the patronage — though in no patronizing sense — of these two related on-going movements in the growth of human consciousness. The Council further undertook the renewal and reform of Christian doctrine and life in the light of these new signs of the times. In particular, the times demand a reconsideration of the classical concept of the ecclesial relationship — a new development, doctrinal and practical, in the relation between authority and freedom in the Church.

The difficulty with the classical conception, as experienced at the moment, is clear enough. It is sometimes stated by saying that obedience is a bar to the self-fulfillment of the individual. The statement may contain a fallacy — an individualistic concept of self-fulfillment, and a failure to realize that self-fulfillment is not simply an affair of freedom but also an affair of community. Briefly, self-fulfillment is the achievement of freedom for communion with the others. Therefore it is also somehow an affair of obedience to authority; for in every kind of community there is always some kind of authority.

The fallacy aside, it must be said that the contemporary difficulty with the classical conception is rooted in a truth — in an experience of the truth that the signs of the times reveal. What is really being said is that sheer submission to the will of the superior and mere execution of his orders do not satisfy the exigencies of the dignity of the person. They do not call into play the freedom of the person at its deepest point, where freedom appears as love. Still less do they exhaust the responsibilities of the person, which are to participate fully in community, and to contribute actively to community. Thus stated, the contemporary difficulty is seen to be entirely valid. It is not to be solved by methods of repression of the principle of authority: that authority is to be obeyed simply because it is authority.

C. *In the Service of the Community*

There is a need, therefore, to view the issue of freedom and authority in the new perspectives created by the signs of the times — that is, to view the issue within the context of community, which is the milieu wherein the dignity of the person is realized. Community is the context both of command and of obedience. Community is also the finality both of command and obedience. Authority is indeed from God, but it is exercised in community over human persons. The freedom of the human person is also from God, and it is to be used in community for the benefit of the others. Moreover, since both authority and freedom stand in the service of the community, they must be related not only vertically but also horizontally, as we shall see.

II. THE CHURCH, A UNIQUE COMMUNITY

It may be well to remark here that there is no univocal definition of the ruler-ruled relationship because there is no univocal definition of community. This latter term is analogous. The realities it designates — the family, political society, voluntary associations, the Church — are somewhat the same and entire-

4

ly different, one from another. In the case of the Church, which is at once a family and a society and a form of voluntary association, the essential thing is to attend to the *maior dissimilitudo*. Within the uniqueness of the Church as a community, the uniqueness of the relation of Christian freedom to ecclesiastical authority comes to view. Happily, Vatican Council II, which raised the issue of freedom and authority in the Church, also created the perspectives within which its resolution becomes newly possible. Four aspects of conciliar ecclesiology are pertinent here.

A. *The Church Is the People of God*

In the first place, the Constitution on the Church (*Lumen gentium*) presents the Church in the first instance as the People of God. The first characteristic of the People is that it "has for its condition the dignity and the freedom of the children of God, in whose hearts the Holy Spirit dwells as in a temple." The basic condition of the People is therefore one of equality in dignity and freedom, established by the common possesion of the Spirit. A consequent characteristic of the People is its charismatic quality as a prophetic, royal and priestly People. The Spirit "distributes special graces among the faithful of every rank, and by these gifts he makes them able and ready to undertake the various tasks and offices useful for the renewal and upbuilding of the Church, according to the Apostle: 'To each is given the manifestation of the Spirit for the common good' (1 Cor. 12-7)." In particular, as the Constitution on Divine Revelation (*Dei Verbum*) says, God through the Spirit "uninterruptibly converses with the Bride of his beloved Son," and the Spirit continually "leads unto all truth those who believe and makes the word of Christ dwell abundantly in them." The dignity of the People and its common endowment of Christian freedom importantly consists in the charismatic quality of its members.

B. *The Church Is a Communion*

In the second place, the Council presents the Church as a communion (*koinonia*). Its infinite inner form is the Holy Spirit Himself, the subsistent love of Father and Son, who is the presence of God in the midst of His People. In consequence, the Church is in the first instance an interpersonal community, whose members are united in love of the Father through Christ and in the Spirit, and also united with one another by the Spirit of Christ, through whom they have access not only to the Father but to one another. The consequence here is one of immense importance, namely, that as an interpersonal community the Church is an end in itself, an ultimate reality, as eschatological reality in a temporal realization thereof. As a communion *sui generis*, the Church has for its primary purpose simply to be a communion. As such it will endure beyond time, forever, in what is called the communion of saints.

C. *The Church Is a Witness to the World*

In the third place, precisely as an interpersonal communion of love, the Church has a service (*diakonia*) to perform toward all humanity. That is to say, the divine love that is the form of the People, is made present in witness (*martyrion*), to draw all men into the communion of love, so that they may participate in the response of faith and love to the love whereby the Father loves His own People, purchased by the blood of His Son. In other words, precisely as an interpersonal community *sui generis*, the Church is also a functional community that is a community with a work to do, an action to perform — the action of God in history, which is to "gather into one the children of God who are scattered abroad" (John 11:52). Moreover, the work of the community, which is a work of love, is not extrinsic to the thematic of the community; it is woven, as it were, into this thematic as an essential element of it. That is to say, the interpersonal community, united in love, is also united by the missionary work of love to which it is called by its very nature.

Regarded as a functional community, however, the Church is not an end in itself but a means to a higher end — its own growing selfrealization and perfection as an interpersonal community. There will come a day when the Messianic function of the Church will have been finished — the Day of the Lord, when the gathering of the People will be complete and the reign of Christ definitively established: "Then comes the end, when he delivers the kingdom to God the Father" (1 Cor. 15:24).

D. *The Church Is a Visible Society*

In the fourth place, the Church is not only a community of faith and love but also a visible society; it therefore exhibits a structure of authority and a juridical order. Moreover, the Church is an organized society precisely as a community of faith and love with a function to perform in history. The societal aspect of the Church is not alien or extrinsic to its communal and functional aspects, but essential to both of them and inherent in each of them. That is to say, the organization of the society is required by the purposes of the community, both for the sake of its own unity as an interpersonal communion and also for the sake of its action in history. The hierarchically ordered society — its structure of authority and its juridical order — stands in the service of the community, to assist in perfecting its unity and in performing its function.

The structure of authority in the Church is unique, as the community it structures is likewise unique. It is both doctrinal and jurisdictional — a power of authoritative teaching and of imperative rule. Moreover, the structure is not merely a matter of political and sociological necessity, as in the case of the civil community. This latter is simply a functional community, which is therefore organized only in order to get its work done — its work being what is called the common good. Here the *maior dissimilitudo* appears. The Church is organized as a society *sui generis*, an interpersonal, eschatological communion of faith and love and a historical, missionary community whose work in history expresses its own inner reality.

6

III. Functions of Authority in the Church

These four themes in the ecclesiology of Vatican II are, of course, entirely traditional. The order of their arrangement, however, is distinctive; so too is the weight of emphasis distributed among them. For Leo XIII, for instance, the Church was both community and society, indissolubly; so it is presented in *Satis Cognitum*. But the weight of his emphasis falls heavily on the societal aspect and on the structure of authority in the Church. It may be fairly, if rather broadly, said that Leo XIII comes to the notion of the Church as community through the notion of the Church as society. And in his construction, the functions of Christian freedom are not readily apparent: they are, in fact, obscured. Authority seems, as it were, to stand over the community as a power to decide and command. In contrast, Vatican II comes to the notion of the Church as society through the notion of the Church as community. Authority therefore stands, as it were, within the community, as a ministry to be performed in the service of the community. Within the perspectives created by this newly accented construction of traditional doctrine, the ecclesial relationship can be more adequately understood and therefore stated with a new nicety of balance. In particular, the functions of Christian freedom emerge into new clarity, in themselves and in their relation to the correspondent functions of authority. The new clarity radiates from the notion of the Church as community, now made newly luminous.

The functions of authority appear to be three, in hierarchical order. And each of them is a function of service to the community.

A. *Unitive Function*

The first function is unitive. Authority is to be and do what God Himself, through Christ and in the Spirit, is and does. He gathers, unites, establishes communion. This too is the primary function of authority. Moreover, God gathers His Church by initiating and sustaining with men the "dialogue of salvation," brilliantly described by Paul VI in *Ecclesiam Suam*. God communicates with His People, eliciting from them the response of faith and love. His call to them is an imperative laid upon them, but it is, in the words of Paul VI, a "demand of love" (*domanda di amore*), to which the response must be free. So, too, authority performs its unitive function through dialogue with the charismatic body of the faithful. The purpose of the ecclesiastical dialogue, as of the divine dialogue is to build and strengthen the community; to guide it, under the guidance of the Spirit, toward the full truth. About what? About itself, in the first instance. The dialogue is to deepen that "self-awareness" on the part of the community which was a major theme, and also a major achievement of Vatican II.

Authority therefore elicits from the charismatic community of Christian faith the insights of each into the faith, for the enlightment of all. (This function receives new emphasis in the new charter of the reformed Congregation for the Doctrine of Faith; it was also strongly advanced in the discourse of Paul

VI on Oct. 1, 1966, to the International Congress on the Theology of Vatican Council II, when he spoke of the reciprocal dependency of the magistery upon the theologian and of the theologian upon the magistery.) Moreover, authority stirs the love of the charismatic members of the community for the community to be shown in service of the community. Finally, authority solicits the informed concern of the community for the work of the community — its relations with the world, its mission of salvation and its spiritual mission in the temporal order. (This function is broadly emphasized all through the Constitution on the Church in the Modern World, as well as in almost all the other conciliar documents.)

The primacy of this unitive function of authority, to be discharged through dialogue, results from the primacy of the notion of the Church as an interpersonal community whose conscious unity is an end in itself. This primary dialogic function also depends for its performance on the reality of the People of God as a charismatic body, whose basic condition is one of equality in Christian dignity and freedom. It follows therefore that the unitive function of authority is to be carried out under respect for this basic condition. *Lumen gentium* is careful to provide room in the Church for all manner of legitimate diversities and pluralisms — in rites, theologies, spiritualities, apostolates, etc. — which, so far from damaging the unity of the community, constitute an enrichment of it. The principle of the Declaration on Religious Freedom — that there should be in society as much freedom as possible and only as much restriction as necessary — applies analogously in the Church. Only "in necessary things" is unity itself necessary.

It may be remarked here that the modes and manners in which authority is to perform its unitive function through dialogue are still problematical today, in this area of *assestamento* (adjustment). New structures of communication need to be created (for instance, the Synod that will meet in 1967). Older structures need reformation, as in the case of the Roman dicasteries. Experiments are called for that will yield the necessary experience. The problem is not simply to conceptualize in theological terms the relation between authority and freedom in the Christian community, as it appears in new perspectives; this relation must be lived, in all concreteness and practicality. Thus the experience of life will give vitality to the theology.

B. *Decisive or Directive Function*

The second function of authority may be called decisive or directive. It hardly needs lengthy description, since it already is a familiar thing, prominent perhaps to the point of undue emphasis in the classical conception of an older day. The decisive function is necessary because the Church is a community of faith, and it was to the magistery that the guardianship of the deposit of the faith was committed. The directive function is needed because the Church is a functional community organized for action in history. It is to be noted, however, that the necessity of the function is not merely a matter of efficiency, to insure that the work of the Church gets done. The necessity is grounded in the very nature of the community. The point is to insure that the work done is the work of the Church which it is when it is done under direction. The even more important point is to insure that the Body acts as one in the action of its members, singly and collectively.

Thus the decisive and directive function of authority is in a true sense a modality of its unitive function. Moreover, the performance of this secondary function supposes that the primary function has already been performed; that the dialogue, whether doctrinal or pastoral, has been afoot between the community and its teachers and pastors; that therefore the decisions and directives, without ceasing to derive their force from apostolic authority, are also the decisions and directives of the community, whose common good they serve.

C. Corrective or Punitive Function

The third function of authority is corrective or punitive. It is an accidental function, in the sense that it is necessary only because the People of God, on its pilgrim way through history is a sinful People. It is also a function of service to the community, which needs to be protected against the egoisms — whether of thought or of action — that would destroy its unity or damage its work. Again, therefore, this function of correction appears as a modality of the unitive function of authority. What comes to the fore today is the need that the corrective or punitive function of authority should be performed under regard for what is called, in the common-law tradition, "due process." The demand for due process of law is an exigence of Christian dignity and freedom. It is to be satisfied as exactly in the Church as in civil society (one might indeed say, more exactly.)

IV. FUNCTIONS OF CHRISTIAN FREEDOM IN THE CHURCH

Three functions of Christian freedom in the Church correspond to the three functions of ecclesiastical authority. They are likewise functions of service to the community.

A. Charismatic Function

The primary function may be called, for the sake of a name, charismatic. It is the free response of the community and of all its members to the unitive function of authority, whose initial act is the invitation to dialogue (on which the Council more than once laid emphasis). The Spirit is given to the Christian not only for his own sanctification and enjoyment, but also for the growth of the community in conscious self-awareness and for the fuller development of its action in history. Concretely, the community uses the gift of the Spirit by sustaining its part in the dialogue with authority, in that confidence of utterance that reveals — in our times, as in those of the Acts of the Apostles — the presence of the Spirit.

9

The primary function of Christian freedom corresponds therefore to the nature of freedom in its most profound sense — to the nature of freedom as love, as the capacity for self-communication, as the spontaneous impulse to minister and not be ministered to, as the outgoing will to communion with the others. "For you were called to freedom, brethren," St. Paul proclaims (Gal. 5:13). Whatever else the call may imply, it is a call to love: ". . . . . . through love to be servants of one another" (loc cit.). The forms of service within the community are manifold, but the primary service to the community is to participate in the dialogue of salvation that is continually going on in the community. This participation is the first exercise of Christian freedom. It is also an exercise in obedience, in the horizontal dimension that obedience assumes when it is situated, with authority, within community, and therefore in dialogic relation to authority, united to authority in a ministry of love toward the community.

B. *Executive Function*

The second function of Christian freedom may be called, again for the sake of a name, executive. It corresponds to the decisive and directive functions of authority. It also corresponds to the formal notion of freedom as duty — the freedom whereby one does what one ought to do. Here, of course, obedience may occasionally appear as self-sacrifice. The act of obedience is not, of course, *per se* an act of sacrifice; it is simply an act of Christian freedom. Obedience assumes a sacrificial quality only when Christian freedom meets the resistance of what Paul calls "the flesh." And the premise of obedience as sacrifice is always the profound nature of freedom as love — the love whereby one freely engages oneself in the paschal mystery. Hence obedience, as an act of Christian freedom, even when it is sacrificial — especially when it is sacrificial — is always the act of self-fulfillment. It is the expression of one's self-awareness that one is called to be in the image of the Son Incarnate, who freely gave His life for the many and thus "went His way" to the self-fulfillment that was His resurrection. Finally, whether sacrificial or not, the executive function of Christian freedom, which consists in acceptance of the decisions and directives of authority, is always performed within the community, in and for which He works. Therefore this secondary function of freedom is related to the primary function, the charismatic function of love whereby I contribute to dialogue to the unity of the communion that is the Church. The dialogue is not an end in itself; it looks towards decisions and directives. In their issuance and acceptance, the community comes together in a new way.

C. *Self-corrective Function*

The third function of Christian freedom may have to go without a name, unless one calls it self-corrective, in order to mark its correspondence to the corrective function of authority. It is the free act of Christian refusal to "submit again to a yoke of slavery" (Gal. 5:1). More broadly, it is the Christian rejection of the temptation, inherent in the psychological notion of freedom as choice, to "use your freedom as an opportunity for the flesh" (Gal. 5:13). One might call it the "mortifying" act of Christian freedom; the word may not be popular today, but the notion is still Pauline (cf. Rom. 8:13). In any event, it is the act whereby Christian freedom stands forth in all its evangelical newness, unique among all the modalities of freedom that men have claimed or hoped for or dreamed of. "It was that we might be free" in this new way, says St. Paul, "that Christ has freed us" (Gal. 5:1).

CONCLUSION

The aim of this brief essay has been simply to suggest how the rather fleshless skeleton of the classical conception of the ecclesial relation may be clothed with flesh and animated with blood. The skeleton remains; the classical conception of the vertical relationship of authority and freedom. But it needs to assume a more Christian and therefore more human form by standing forth in the living flesh and blood that is the Christian community. More abstractly, the vertical relationship of command-obedience needs to be completed by the horizontal relationship of dialogue between authority and the free Christian community. The two relationships do not cancel, but reciprocally support, each other.

This more adequate understanding of the ecclesial relationship does not indeed dissolve the inevitable tension between freedom and authority. But by situating this perennial polarity within the living context of community, it can serve to make the tension healthy and creative, releasing the energies radiant from both poles for their one common task, which is to build the beloved community.

JOHN COURTNEY MURRAY, S.J.

This article first appeared in *America* of December 3, 1966 and was also included in *We, The People of God . . .*, ed. James A. Coriden (Huntington, IN: Our Sunday Visitor and C.L.S.A., 1968).

APPROACHING THE REVISED CODE

Approaching the revised Code can be compared to approaching a new wine. We know it comes from historic soil, tested vines, and an estate with experience in producing this kind of thing. Yet still we approach it carefully, first sipping to get the initial taste; then savoring a second sip to discover the nuance. Finally, we must decide how to store and, eventually, consume the product.

So it is with the recently promulgated revised Code. Its roots extend back through Christian tradition to the Scriptures themselves. It comes from centuries of legal tradition within the Catholic community. The revised Code itself is the product of a complicated process conducted on behalf of the Holy See and reaching out for consultation with bishops and experts from around the world. But what is the final product like? Let me share a first sip with you, and then a more nuanced taste. Finally, let me suggest some possibilities for receiving the revised Code in this country.

An Overview

Influence of Vatican II

When John XXIII called for an "aggiornamento" of the Code of Canon Law twenty-four years ago this year, he saw it as a way of implementing in the practical life of the Church the renewal he was inaugurating in the Catholic Church. In many ways the revised Code is remarkably faithful to the decisions of Second Vatican Council, the touchstone of John's renewal.

The revised law provides a common status for all in the Church, based on their baptism and directed toward their involvement in the mission of the Church. The distinctions of clergy and laity remain, but are placed in a new context. Instead of building the whole legal structure on the differences between clergy and laity as the 1917 Code did, this revised law begins with the common dignity of all the baptized and puts distinctions in terms of service and ministry. Responsibilities and rights of all Christians are spelled out in what for canon law is a new experience of a kind of "bill of rights." Theoretically, involvement in Church work is open to any Christian provided the person has the necessary qualifications. The special responsibilities that arise from one's state in life, for example, parenthood, are given explicit recognition.

The role of lay persons receives increased attention in the Code, as it did in Vatican II. Their responsibility for spreading the Gospel in every walk of life is recalled. Their rights to the spiritual goods of the Church, especially the Word of God and the sacraments, form the basis for several innovations in how ministry is to be structured, and even the variety of persons who may perform official Church ministry.

One of the major issues at Vatican II was the relationship of the diocesan bishops with Rome. The collegiality of bishops and the role of the diocesan bishop within his local church were major advances of the Council. These are reflected in many striking ways in the revised Code. The local bishop has considerable freedom of action. Many restrictions on his initiative and discretion have been removed and he is encouraged to apply the law to the local conditions of his church, always working within the framework of the Code and directives from the Vatican.

As he does this, the bishop is called to a renewed sense of Church as a community of persons rather than his own fiefdom or possession. Applying the people-centered definition of a diocese which comes from Vatican II, the revised Code extends this approach to its definition of a parish. No longer just an administrative division of the diocese, as it could be considered under the old Code, the parish is now presented as a community of persons with their own life and mission. The assignment of clergy, development of programs, and determination of membership in parish communities is more flexible under the revised law, but is to fit within the general framework of this communitarian approach. If there are not enough priests to have a resident pastor in each parish, for example, the parish need not be closed; a person who is not a priest, whether a deacon, a religious or lay woman or man, can be given the daily pastoral care within that community.

Compromise

If the revised Code is faithful to Vatican II, it is also faithful to one of the key experiences of the Council as well: compromise. The document is clearly a compromise on many issues debated at the Council, or debated even before then among canon lawyers. For example, at Vatican II the role of episcopal conferences was hotly debated. Some saw it as a weakening of the role of the local bishop; others, as a threat to the role of the Holy See. Still, episcopal conferences were set up and have proven to be a major benefit to the life of the Church in many areas of the world.

The revised Code keeps the episcopal conference structure, and calls on conferences to set policy in a variety of issues. But the revision process reflected the same tensions over the role of the conferences and the law shows the results of this compromise. The conference can bind local dioceses in only a few matters. On the other hand, they are free to develop a spirit of mutual understanding and cooperation, and can continue to develop as major influences in the life of the Church. What is in the law does not exhaust the possibilities of what can become effective through creative action.

Marriage tribunal procedures are another example of compromise. Many of the advances contained in the American Procedural Norms have now been extended to the Church universal. On the other hand, the requirement that every case be reviewed by a panel of three judges has been reimposed on the Church courts in this country. Dioceses across the nation are now exploring ways to live with this compromise.

A third area of compromise concerns Church finances. The revised Code does not address the Vatican's finances. Presumably, those are governed by special norms for the Roman Curia and the Vatican City State. The Code's laws do affect local dioceses, however, and show the influence of a debate over the most appropriate way to fund diocesan operations. The Code Commission's secretariat argued that the canonical traditional puts first emphasis on free-will offerings of the faithful. Many American dioceses do rely heavily on this, whether through an annual fund drive or by more sophisticated long-term giving programs of annuities and wills. But a number of the Code Commission members, primarily diocesan bishops themselves, wanted to regularize a practice which is also common in this country whereby dioceses tax a percentage of parish income. This, under the revised Code, will finally become legal in Church law.

Problem Areas

If the Code is marked by compromises, it is also plagued with some issues which may become problems for the Church in the United States. The most publicly noted one is the question of "mandate" for teachers of theology in colleges and universities. The European mentality, rooted in close Church-state relations where the government pays the teachers but the Church retains control over who is named to teach, has predominated in the approach to Catholic higher education even though a majority of the world's Catholic institutions of learning are in this country. Ways of working with this new law are being explored with civil law experts.

Another problem area is the role of consultative bodies such as priests' councils, diocesan pastoral councils, and parish councils. The revised Code can be read as giving the bishop (or pastor, at the parish level) a much more controlling role in these bodies than is congenial to the American experience. The struggles of the years since the Council to implement what many rightly understood as shared responsibility and a greater role for priests and lay persons in the life of the Church could be lost if the revised Code is not interpreted very carefully.

A third problem could be hiding in the law on the sale of Church property. While it does not change radically the previous practice, it does clarify some aspects of the law which were mercifully vague heretofore, and might cause religious communities and various Church institutions some additional headaches in today's business climate.

Beneath these more immediate aspects of the revised Code there are some challenging nuances which deserve to be addressed. Like savoring a wine, there are bitter and sweet impressions when studying this document.

Law for Disciples

It is, underneath all its traditional language and legal formulation, an attempt to develop a law for disciples. A lot of the restrictive details of the former Code have been done away with. The role of penalties or sanctions in Church law has been dramatically reduced. Although procedures for accountability do exist, teeth to enforce them are lacking or relatively weak. Local adaptation is stressed, although with caution.

What this means is that if the revised Code is going to work, it will be because it is accepted by a faith community which sees in it an instrument to promote its following of the Lord. Rather than a set of laws for a government to enforce, this Code is intended as a discipline for a people who are themselves committed to discipleship.

If a Church official is not a person of faith, this law could be circumvented, obstructed, or ignored. For a community more interested in power politics than proclaiming the Word, the law can be a source of frustration or even alienation. This is a risk the revisers of the Code decided to take, for it is the risk the Council (and Christ!) have invited us to undertake. Disciples are called to faith, not lording it over others.

New Way of Thinking

Perhaps this illustrates a second nuance in the revised Code. It is an attempt to reflect a new way of thinking, that "new habit of mind" which Paul VI charged the Code Commission to implement when he set them upon their task at the conclusion of Vatican II. A new way of thinking takes time to absorb, for when we deal with law we deal with a very conservative aspect of life and often we miss the nuance this new way of thinking requires.

A first expression of this new thinking is in the whole understanding of the Church which is reflected in the Code. The 1917 Code clearly addressed the Church as a monarchy, a religious government with institutions stretching from the universal to the most local neighborhood levels. The revised Code attempts to take seriously the sense of Church as a communion, a bonding together of people in the Lord and with one another at various levels of their Church experience. Many of the structures of the old Code are still there, but the attempt has been made to address them in a new context.

Another expression of the new way of thinking is in the approach to ministry. Church office is no longer restricted just to clergy. The rights of the faithful to the Word and sacraments can lead to lay people staffing parishes, parents exercising greater responsibility in preparing their children for Christian life, and the whole community getting involved in marriage preparation.

Empowerment of the Church to carry out the three-fold work of Christ, teaching, sanctifying and transforming the world to his rule, is as central to this Code as the restrictive controls were to the 1917 version.

A third impact of the new way of thinking is how the revised law deals with other Christians. In the 1917 law, they were considered "bad Catholics," bound by the restrictions of the Catholic Church's law but not able to benefit from rights within the Church. The revised Code is more realistic. Other Christians are other Christians, not bad Catholics. They are not bound by the restrictions in Catholic Church law, but are able to benefit from a number of rights within the Church if they so desire — for example, the right to hear the Word preached, or to receive certain sacraments under conditions which respect ecumenical sensitivities and our own tradition.

Challenge and Opportunity

As a law for disciples and a new way of thinking, the revised Code is an important opportunity for the Church everywhere, including in this country. What we do with that opportunity, however, may well determine whether we have caught these nuances. The revision process at the Vatican illustrates how difficult it can be to think anew as disciples.

The Code has been revised in a rather unique system, covered by secrecy which is designed to leak, consulting bishops around the world but influenced by politics with civil governments and political pressures within the Church structure. It was ostensibly the work of a commission, but a commission whose members were often too occupied elsewhere to spend quality time working on the product, and many of whose members are removed from pastoral life. The final product was reexamined by the pope and a select group of advisors who remained anonymous, a process subject to much intrigue and pressure. The idea of consultation was good, but the practice illustrates how hard it is to adopt a new way of thinking while immersed in system which served the old as well.

What about ourselves? Will the opportunity to implement Vatican II's renewal in the very legal structures of the Church bring forth a new way of doing this, recognizing the common dignity and responsibility of all disciples? Or, will we slip into the old way of doing things, leaving it up to the "experts," the bishops and their staffs or the episcopal conference, to determine how the implementation is to be done? There are a number of practical decisions to be made, adaptations of the law to be worked out, and structures to be evaluated and revised.

The revised Code continues the ancient Christian tradition of making laws in synods and councils. But it also provides for administrative decrees which bishops can issue on their own, with or without consulting anyone. Only in a very few cases must the bishop consult with specified groups before issuing a decision. The opportunity in this new way of thinking is for bishops and the bishops' conference to take advantage of the possibilities as we have never been able to do it before, and to make the implementation of the revised Code an experience of discipleship.

New wine should not be put into old wine skins. It takes a new skin, if it is not to burst the old and be lost. Something similar applies to the revised Code. The new way of thinking, the opportunity for discipleship, takes more than the old way of doing things if it will survive and meet the expectations that marked John XXIII's call for the revised Code.

There has been a kind of anti-nominanism since the Council, an attitude that law had no place in Church life. People have been alienated by outmoded procedures, or experiences in which their expectations for new life were dashed by an authority's appeal to old legalisms. The attitude toward the revised Code has often been one of "ho-hum," or a bemused look at stewards rearranging deck chairs on the Titanic.

Recently, I have discovered new interest in Church law. A group of theology students reported at the end of last semester they were amazed at how pastoral and creative the revised Code can be. During a series of workshops on the revised Code for diocesan administrators, the experience was repeated over and over of people awakening to the fact that this is not a law of "musts," but really is a new way of thinking. It does hold promise for promoting the pastoral life of the Church and setting the stage for more dynamic mission by the Catholic community.

The difference lies in our attitude. Disciples are not timid; they seek to follow the master in new and uncharted lands. Yet they remain faithful to his teaching, disciplining themselves even as they challenge others to convert and join them. So are we in approaching this revised Code. We must not be timid in seeking a more creative approach to its implementation, to the development of those new wine skins that are so necessary if the nuance and promise of this Code is to be captured. But true to the Lord's teaching, our new way of thinking must again lead us to that Gospel which is ever old and ever new, and out of whose treasures we continually seek to bring both the new and the old.

JAMES H. PROVOST, JCD
Washington, DC

This article first appeared in *America*, February 5, 1983.

COMPARISION OF CODES

THE THREE-FOLD *MUNERA* OF CHRIST AND THE CHURCH

Canon 204 of the new law states that "the faithful participate in the priestly, prophetic and royal *munus* of Christ."

The word *munus* is difficult to translate: sometimes it is translated as "office" or "role," sometimes as "mission" or "service," and sometimes as "ministry," particularly in the United States, where the word "ministry" has taken on such a wide meaning. The doctrine of the three-fold *munera*, originally a Christology, was translated into an ecclesiology by the Second Vatican Council, and many of the documents of the Council are structured in terms of these three offices or ministries. The Code of Canon Law has been similarly influenced by this doctrine.

Each of the three pivotal chapters of the Constitution on the Church *Lumen gentium* treat of the three-fold *munera*.

Chapter Two — The People of God — presents the people of God as a priestly people. A distinction is made between the common priesthood of the faithful and the ministerial or hierarchical priesthood (LG 10, 11). The people of God share in Christ's prophetic office. The whole body of the faithful cannot err in matters of belief; they have "sensus fidei." Moreover, the people of God have special graces or charisms fitting them for their various tasks or offices (LG 12). Finally, the people of God are a kingdom, not of this earth (LG 13).

In Chapter Three on the Hierarchical Church, references to both the role of bishops and the role of presbyters are divided in accordance with the three-fold *munera*.

The bishops have a mission of teaching, wherein preaching the Gospel has pride of place (LG 24, 25). Bishops are stewards of the grace of the Supreme Priest. Churches, as Eucharistic communities, are presided over by bishops (LG 26). And the bishops govern the churches, having pastoral charge over them (LG 27). Similarly, presbyters are associated with bishops to preach the Gospel, to shepherd the faithful, and to celebrate divine worship (LG 28).

Finally, Chapter Four on the Laity is similarly structured. The laity share the priestly, prophetic and kingly office of Christ (LG 31). They have a priestly office (LG 34), they have a prophetic office and a responsibility to share in evangelization (LG 35), and the kingdom of justice, love and peace is spread by the lay faithful (LG 36).

The document on the role of bishops *Christus Dominus* further develops the concept of the three-fold *munera*: the bishop's teaching office, including preaching, catechetical instruction, doctrinal instruction in schools and public statements (CD 12, 13, 14); his sanctifying role (CD 15); and his pastoral role, including building community among the clergy, ecumenical dialogue, coordinating the apostolate, seeing to the special needs of people (CD 16, 17, 18).

Similarly, the document on presbyters deals with the three-fold office of a presbyter (*Presbyterorum ordinis*). The presbyter is a minister of God's Word (PO 4), a minister of the sacraments and the Eucharist (PO 5), and pastor and ruler of God's people (PO 6).

Finally, the document on the Apostolate of the Laity has a similar three-fold structure (*Apostolicam actuositatem*). The laity are made to share in the priestly, prophetical and kingly office of Christ (AA 2). The objectives of the lay apostolate include the apostolate of evangelzation and sanctification (AA 6), the renewal of the temporal order (AA 7), and charitable works and social aid (AA 8). Moreover, the laity have a special role in church communities, acting as priest, prophet or king, taking part in parish and diocesan apostolates of evangelization, catechetical instruction and even assistance in the care of souls and the administration of Church property (AA 10).

Two of the books in the new Code, originally listed under *Res* in the 1917 Code, are now structured in accordance with the ecclesiological doctrine of the three *munera*, namely the book on the *munus docendi*, and the book on the *munus sanctificandi*. Even the Vatican Council was ambiguous regarding the significance of the *munus regendi*. This *munus* includes the ministry of government, but is certainly not limited to that, since a reading of the Vatican II texts clearly shows that the *munus* includes the entire pastoral office and not just governance in the canonical sense. In fact, from the standpoint of the lay apostolate, the *munus* extends even to the transformation of the temporal order, and the Church's commitment to spiritual and corporal works of mercy. Because of this ambiguity, several reasons are given for neglecting a book on the *munus regendi*.

1. Since the *munus regendi* includes the ministry of governance, the entire Code deals with the function or ministry.
2. From the standpoint of the lay apostolate and the transformation of social order, the *munus regendi* must be left to the particular church by reason of the doctrine of subsidiarity. It is only the particular church that can make adequate decisions regarding this aspect of the *munus regendi*.
3. Even interpreting the *munus regendi* as pastoral care suggests that much legislation needs to be left to the particular church, although one could say that the *munus regendi* is death with in many sections of Book Two on the People of God.
4. Finally, the *munus regendi* includes the administration of temporalities for the sake of worship, ministry and the care of the poor, and from this point of view, Book Five on Church Property deals with some of the issues of this *munus regendi*.

BERTRAM F. GRIFFIN, JCD
Portland, Oregon

THE AGES OF MAN

Jacques defines the seven ages of man as
   1. the infant, mewling and puking in the nurse's arms;
   2. and then the whining school boy . . . creeping like snail, unwillingly, to school;
   3. and then the lover, sighing like a furnace;
   4. then a soldier, full of strange caths . . . seeking the bubble reputation, even in the cannon's mouth;
   5. then the justice in fair round belly with good capon lined, . . . full of wise saws and modern instances;
   6. in the sixth age, one shifts into the lean and slippered pantaloon, with spectacles on nose and pouch on side;
   7. the last scene of all is second childishness and mere oblivion sans teeth, sans eyes, sans taste, sans everything.

(*As You Like It*, Act II,
scene 6, lines 140 and following)

The new Code on Canon Law, perhaps less descriptively, also speaks of seven ages of man: infants, children, youth, young adults, mature adults, older adults, and retired ministers.

   1. Infants. Infancy extends until the age of reason, or discretion. One is presumed to have attained the age of reason at the age of seven (canon 97, §2).

Infants are to be baptized within the first few weeks of life (canon 867, §1).

   2. Children. Children are minors who are no longer infants, but who also do not have some of the rights of those young people who are still not considered adult. The age of childhood could be considered to stretch from the age of seven to the age of fourteen or sixteen. Certainly with the age of seven it is presumed that the child has left infancy.

Children who have reached the age of reason fall under the norms regarding adult baptism (canon 852, §). The age of discretion is the usual age for confirmation, unless the episcopal conference decides on another age (canon 891). With the use of reason, children begin preparation for First Communion and celebrate First Communion as soon as they can (canon 914). Once children reach the age of discretion, they are required to confess their grave sins at least once a year (canon 989). Finally, with the use of reason, children can receive the sacrament of anointing of the sick (canon 1004, §1).

Having reached the use of reason, children can obtain a quasi-domicile (canon 105, §1). Infants and children under the age of fourteen follow the ritual transfer of their parents, but may return to the Latin Rite after that age (canon 111).

3. Youth. Youth could be said to begin with the age of fourteen or sixteen since special rights and obligations begin at those ages.

At the age of fourteen, one is free to choose one's own rite of baptism (canon 111, §2). Beginning with the age of fourteen, catechumens who wish to be baptized should be referred to the bishop (canon 863). Girls may validly marry at the age of fourteen; boys are restricted until the age of sixteen from valid marriage (canon 1083). With the age of fourteen, young people are bound by the law of abstinence (canon 1252).

At the age of sixteen, one can become a sponsor for baptism and confirmation (canon 874). With the age of sixteen, young people are bound by the law of ecclesiastical sanctions (canon 1323).

Prior to the age of eighteen, infants, children and young people (minors) are subject to their parents or tutors (canon 98) and retain the domicile and quasi-domicile of their parents or tutors (canon 105) (although, as we mentioned above, children over the age of seven can obtain their own quasi-domicile). Minors also must be represented before Church courts by their parents or tutors (canon 1478).

Prior to becoming adults at the age of eighteen, young people, even though capable of valid marriage, are still considered minors and may not marry if their parents are reasonably unwilling (canon 1071). Moreover, the episcopal conference can establish a higher age for liceity than the age of valid marriage (canon 1083, §2).

4. Young Adults. With the age of eighteen, one enters adulthood in the Church.

When one becomes an adult at the age of eighteen, one is bound to the law of fast on Ash Wednesday and Good Friday (canon 1252).

With the age of eighteen, one can make a valid temporary profession (canon 656) and therefore, must be at least seventeen years old for valid entrance into the novitiate of a religious institute (canon 643). Eighteen years is required for initial probation for entering a secular institute (canon 721) and commitments to a society of apostolic life cannot validly be made prior to the age of majority. Hence, young people may validly enter a novitiate at the age of seventeen (canon 735 and 643).

With the age of eighteen, young adults can act as advocates or procurators in Church courts (canon 1483) and, as mentioned above, can stand in Church court on their own without parents or tutors (canon 1478).

5. Mature Adults. Certain rights and privileges can be exercised by adults who are somewhat more mature than the age of eighteen.

You may not make valid perpetual profession until the age of twenty-one.

You must be twenty-three years old before ordination to the transitional diaconate and twenty-five before ordination to the priesthood. You must be 25 before you can be ordained to the permanent celibate diaconate and thirty-five before the married permanent diaconate (canon 1031).

You must be thirty years old before you can be appointed a judicial vicar or an associate judicial vicar (canon 1420), a vicar general or an episcopal vicar (canon 478).

And you must be thirty-five years of age and at least five years as a presbyter before you can be nominated as a bishop (canon 378).

6. Older members of the Church. With the age of sixty, one is no longer obliged to fast (canon 1252).

Diocesan bishops are asked to submit their resignations at the age of seventy-five (canon 401) and pastors are also asked to submit their resignations at the age of seventy-five (can 538).

Cardinals are also requested to submit their resignations at the age of seventy-five. However, once they reach the age of eighty, there are certain required limitations of their rights and prerogatives. They are required to retire as members of the Curia. The 1980 schema had reflected the present discipline that they are not permitted to participate in the election of a Pope, but the October, 1981 consultation recommended that this matter be referred to papal norms.

7. Retirement. This ends this strange, eventful history. I've been able to find no references in the proposed Canon law to that "last scene of all — second childishness and mere oblivion — sans teeth, sans eyes, sans taste, sans everything" — with the possible exception of those canons directing the episcopal conference to establish norms for the pensions of retired bishops (canon 402) and pastors (canon 538).

Bertram F. Griffin, JCD
Portland, Oregon

PARTICULAR LEGISLATION

A. *What is particular legislation?*

A *law* is a general norm established for the common good of a specific community by competent authority.

When a law applies to the entire Latin rite Church it is termed "universal"; when it applies to a smaller community, whether by territorial or by personal determination, it is termed "particular."

Promulgation is the moment when a law begins to exist.

B. *How is a particular law promulgated?*

The method of promulgation is left to the legislator (c. 8). If the legislator does not indicate the *vacatio legis* it is understood to be one month from the moment of promulgation. Normally, the legislator should specify precisely when the law goes into effect. The *vacatis legis* for the 1983 Code is until November 27, 1983, the first Sunday of Advent.

C. *Who is a legislator in the Church?*

1. The Roman Pontiff and the College of Bishops possess full and supreme power in the Church (c. 331). Besides universal laws, the supreme authority of the Church may also pass laws which pertain only to certain territories or specific groups of Catholics. The *American Procedural Norms* were an example.

2. The diocesan bishop possesses legislative authority for the portion of God's people committed to his care (c. 391). Even when laws are formulated in a synod, the diocesan bishop is considered the sole legislator (c. 466).

3. Councils of Bishops are also legislators in the Church:
   a. regional (national) councils (c. 439)
   b. provincial councils (c. 440).

In such councils all of the bishops who vote legislate collegially: diocesan bishops, coadjutor bishops, auxiliary bishops, and other active titular bishops. Retired bishops may also be called to council and vote (c. 443).

The decrees of the councils of bishops must be reviewed and recognized by Rome (c. 446).

4. Episcopal Conferences may pass legislative decrees but are more restricted in doing so. They may do so only when the "ius commune"

authorizes them or when they receive a petitioned or *motu proprio* mandate from the Apostolic See. In such matters, the law must be passed by ⅔ majority and be reviewed and recognized by Rome (c. 455).

5. The chapters of religious institutes are to pass laws which affect the members of the institute (c. 631). The particular law of a religious institute is extremely important in the revised Code. It consists in the institute's Constitution and in its Directory of statutes (c. 587).

D. Who are bound by diocesan laws?

Diocesan laws (and other particular laws) are presumed to be territorial in nature unless otherwise indicated. They bind therefore all of those who possess a domicile or quasi-domicile as long as they are actually present in the diocese (cc. 12-13).

Those visiting from another diocese are bound only by laws affecting public order, regulating the proper solemnities of acts, or affecting permanent structures (e.g., a sanctuary).

Those without any domicile or quasi-domicile are bound by all the particular laws of the diocese in which they find themselves.

E. What forms do particular laws take in a diocese?

1 Synodal laws (c. 460) are laws for the diocese.

2. General decrees are also laws and must be passed by the diocesan bishop himself (c. 29).

3. Customs become laws after being observed over a period of 30 years (c. 26).

4. General executory decrees can be passed by all with executive authority and may sometimes appear to be laws in themselves. More properly, they are detailed determinations of how laws are to be applied and observed. They are, however, promulgated and have a *vacatio legis* (c. 31).

5. Authoritative interpretation of a law can be given by the legislator and these are sometimes viewed as laws in themselves, particularly in a confusing matter (c. 16).

6. Most particular laws are disciplinary in nature (in the technical sense) but the diocesan bishop can also pass inhabilitating and irritating laws as well. In such cases the requisites or conditions for validity should be explicitly stated (cc. 14-15).

7. The legislator on the diocesan level may not delegate his legislative authority except in cases specified in law. Nevertheless, from a practical point of view, his reliance on consultation may often amount to the same thing (c. 135).

8. No law passed by a legislator with less than supreme authority may be contrary to laws passed by his superior. The same holds true for instructions which attempt to explain and draw out the meaning of higher laws. Insofar as they are contrary, they do not bind (cc. 135; 34).

9. The phrase "particular law" is a very general one and may encompass many different types of norms with various authors and diverse levels of obligation. In drafting such norms, it is important to clarify these points as much as possible.

F. *What are some models for drafting and passing particular law?*
1. The Executive Model

Historically, many diocesan norms have resulted from this type of process. Administrators propose to the diocesan bishop various rules and regulations which are sent out to constituencies by letter.

This can be an efficient method of producing needed norms. In general, however, this limited form of "professional" drafting should be limited to issues which are normally found in general executory decrees.

One forum for this model might be found in the figure of the episcopal council mentioned in Book II (cc. 473; 407).

2. The Conciliar Model

We have had much experience in drafting norms in the Vatican Council, in provincial councils and in the work of Episcopal Conferences. Theoretically, this is not done on the diocesan level since the diocesan bishop is the sole legislator but there is nothing to prevent a bishop from adopting this collegial style of action. The conciliar model draws together legislators and consultants from the entire people of God. It drafts and redrafts documents until a final form is achieved which wins a consensus. The rules for particular councils in the revised Code are helpful in describing this experience. Not only are the various bishops convoked but the following are also called to council: vicars general and vicars episcopal; major superiors; rectors of Catholic Universities and their Deans of Theology and Canon Law; rectors of seminaries. On the provincial level, there are also delegates of pastoral and presbyteral councils (c. 443).

3. The Synodal Model (cc. 460-468)

The diocesan synod is the traditional canonical method of diocesan legislation. The revised Code has changed little in this regard. In many ways, however, it shares the advantages of the conciliar model although in this case there is no deliberative voting since the bishop is seen as the sole legislator. Nevertheless, it is interesting to see the persons who must be called and can be called to participate in the diocesan synod (c. 463).

Diocesan synods must be held only when the diocesan bishop, after consultation with the presbyteral council, judges them to be warranted by circumstances (c. 461). Their decrees are not sent to Rome (c. 467).

4. The Pastoral and Presbyteral Council Model

The pastoral council is optional since the canons speak of its existence in dioceses in which pastoral conditions warrant it (c. 511).

The presbyteral council and college of consultors are mandatory for all dioceses (c. 495).

Both councils offer another style of drafting particular law through representative consultation on a lesser scale than that of the synod. Both are strictly consultative in nature although a close working relationship between the bishop and his council(s) may in practice produce a broad model of governance, at least in the area of policy and norms (cc. 500; 514).

5. The Religious Chapter Model

Religious institutes have undergone a lengthy and sometimes painful juridical reorganization during the past decade or so. They have been involved in redrafting their Constitutions and Directories on a vast scale. As free associations of the faithful, they have had to discover many ways of eliciting the consensus of the community for the drafting of documents which would clarify their very identity and their basic structures of governance and discipline. Various institutes have approached this task in different ways. Canon lawyers can look upon religious who have shared this experience as valuable resources for guidance in developing particular law for the diocese by pointing the way to successful processes of drafting law.

6. The Revision of the Code Model

Since the Vatican Council we have seen the Code of universal laws revised and redrafted. The process involved:
    a. initial groups to develop primary drafts of revised law;
    b. widespread consultation with bishops, major superiors and academic groups;
    c. small groups collating animadversions, consulting and revising the primary drafts;
    d. written animadversions and revisions in dialogue with an international commission;
    e. plenary sessions of the international commission;
    f. individual consultation by the Pope and the commission staff in the final stages.

This model might be fruitful in constructing a diocesan method of drafting particular law without requiring the convocation of large gatherings.

JOHN A. ALESANDRO, JCD
Rockville Centre, New York

A BILL OF RIGHTS AND FREEDOMS

There were fourteen rights and freedoms listed in the *Lex Eclesial Fundamentalis*. Since the Lex is not being published, the October consultation recommended that these rights and freedoms be transferred to Book Two of the Latin Code. The revised Code contains an expanded list of eighteen rights.

1. The fundamental equality of all Christians based on baptism, and equality and dignity in action; the right and freedom to cooperate in building up the Body of Christ (c. 208).
2. The right to evangelize the nations (c. 211).
3. The right to petition, that is, to make known to pastors one's needs (especially spiritual) and one's hopes (c. 212, §2).
4. The right to recommend: the right to advise pastors regarding the good of the church, and to participate in public opinion and informing the faithful (c. 212, §3).
5. The right to receive the Word of God and the sacraments from pastors (c. 213).
6. The right to participate in worship in accordance with legitimate norms of one's own rite (c. 214).
7. The right to one's proper spirituality (c. 214).
8. The right to association: the right to found and direct associations with charitable purposes and as an expression of Christian vocation (c. 215).
9. The right to assembly: the right to hold meetings for the same purpose as to associate (c. 215).
10. The right to promote the apostolate and to one's own proper initiative in apostolic work, based on the right to participate in the Church's mission (c. 216).
11. The right to Christian education (c. 217).
12. Academic freedom: the right to research and to publication (c. 218).
13. Freedom from force in choosing one's station in life (c. 219).
14. The right to a good name and reputation (c.220).
15. Privacy: The right to have others respect what is intimate to one's self (c. 220).

16. The right to vindicate one's rights in Church court and to defend one's rights in Church court (c. 221, §1) with equity and in accordance with law (c. 221, §2).
17. The right to be judged.
18. The right to legality regarding sanctions, that is, the right to expect the Church to impose sanctions only in accordance with law (c. 221, §3).

Precepts of the Church

In addition, there are nine basic precepts listed in this same section of the Code.
1. To maintain communion with the Church and fulfill one's Christian duties (c. 209).
2. To lead a holy life, and to promote the growth and holiness of the Church (c. 210).
3. To evangelize the nations, to announce the divine gift of salvation to all peoples, of every place and time (c. 211).
4. To obey Church authority, both teaching authority and governmental authority (c. 212).
5. At times, to express one's opinion about what is for the good of the Church (c. 212, §3).
6. The obligation of parents to educate their children and to provide Christian education (c. 226, §2).
7. The obligation to promote social justice in keeping with the Church's teaching (c. 222, §2).
8. The obligation to care for the needs of the poor from one's own resources (c. 222, §2).
9. Finally, the ubiquitous precept to support the Church for the purposes of worship, the support of ministers and the works of the apostolate and charity (c. 222, §1).

The rights and freedoms are not stated as clearly and simply as in the above list. The Common Law tradition assumes that my rights and freedoms stop where your rights and freedoms begin. Hence, the Bill of Rights is a very simple and clear statement of the fundamental rights and freedoms. It is the business of the courts to establish the balance between rights and obligations. In the Roman Law and canonical traditional, it is the business of the legislator to spell out these restrictions, and the new Code does so somewhat over-generously.

Canon 223, §1 states that the exercise of rights is limited by considerations of the common good, the rights of others and obligation toward others. Canon 223, §2 states that, in view of the common good, Church authority can regulate and moderate rights and restrict them by laws on invalidity or ineligibility.

Beyond these two restrictions, the rights and freedoms themselves are stated in a way that seems limited to someone coming from the Common Law tradition. Over and over again occur phrases like "according to one's proper condition and role . . . taking into account knowledge and competence . . . taking into account the integrity of faith and morals . . . taking into account the common good . . . taking into account the dignity of persons . . . unless reserved, uniquely to Church authority . . . preserving due reverence for the magisterium . . .," etc.

Rights, Freedoms and Eligibility of the Laity

The preceding section dealt with the general rights and freedoms of all the faithful, both ordained ministers and the laity. There follows a section of the specific rights, freedoms and eligibilities of the laity themselves.

Regarding rights and freedoms -

1. The laity's right to participate in evangelization, both individually and corporately is reaffirmed (c. 225).
2. The laity have all civil freedoms of other citizens (c. 227).
3. The laity have the right to education appropriate for living the Christian life, for evangelizing and defending the faith, and for participating in the apostolate. Moreover, they have the right to enter upon academic studies (c. 229).
4. The laity who are hired as Church ministers have a right to a living wage (c. 231).

Moreover, the laity are eligible for certain sharing in the official ministry of the Church.

1. They are eligible to share in the Church's pastoral ministry and in decision-making (c. 228).
2. They are eligible to receive the mandate to teach a sacred science (c. 229, §3).
3. They are eligible for certain liturgical ministries. These include the stable and installed ministries of lector and acolyte mentioned in *Ministeria Quaedam*, as well as temporary ministries of lector, commentator, cantor, etc. It should be noted that the Code retains the sexist discrimination of *Ministeria Quaedam,,* limiting the stable and installed ministry of lector and acolyte to men only. This is the only example I can find of sexist discrimination in the new Code. Clearly, the temporary ministries of lector, extraordinary minister of the Eucharist, etc., and all other liturgical ministries are not so sexually biased. When ecclesial necessity requires it, and in accordance with law, lay people are eligible to exercise the ministry of the Word, to preside over liturgical prayer, to baptize, and to distribute Holy Communion (c. 230).

Regarding the ministry of the Word, canon 759 reminds us that by virtue of their baptism and confirmation, the laity can be called to exercise the ministry of the Word in cooperation with the bishop and his presbyters. The ordinary preacher is the bishop, the presbyter and the deacon. The laity can be admitted to preach in cases of necessity, or even utility in particular cases, in accordance with norms to be established by the episcopal conference (c. 766). And, of course, the laity shall willingly assist the pastor in the ministry of catechetics (c. 776).

Presiding over liturgical prayer is not specifically mentioned in the new Code, but is rather a matter of liturgical law in the ritual. Canon 1168 does mention that the laity can administer certain sacramentals in the judgment of the ordinary and in accordance with the liturgical books.

The ordinary minister of baptism is the bishop, presbyter or deacon. If the ordinary minister is absent or impeded, a catechist or other lay person deputed by the ordinary can administer baptism (c. 861). This is over and above the traditional doctrine that any person can baptize in danger of death.

The ordinary minister of Communion is the bishop, presbyter or deacon. In case of necessity or pastoral utility, an acolyte or other lay person deputed by the ordinary in accordance with law can also administer the Eucharist (c. 910).

Finally, there is a rather restricted permission in the new law, allowing laity to act as an official witness of marriage. As we know, the ordinary and the pastor are the ordinary witnesses of marriage; both can delegate other priests and deacons. The extraordinary minister (when a priest or deacon is lacking) is a lay person, if the diocesan bishop approves, the episcopal conference votes to allow such an institute, and finally, faculty or indult is obtained from the Holy See (c. 1112).

Other examples of lay participation in ecclesiastical offices include:

1. In tribunal matters, a lay person can be appointed an assessor or judge in a collegiate tribunal. A lay person can be appointed defender of the bond and auditor. In chancery matters, the finance manager and the chancellor can both be lay people.

2. On the parish level, laity can participate as a member of the parish staff with the pastor, or as a member of a parish pastoral team, to whom a parish is entrusted, with a neighboring pastor being the moderator and official pastor.

3. On the other hand, some offices which seemingly do not demand the exercise of priestly powers are still restricted to bishops and presbyters, for example, episcopal vicars, area vicars, judicial vicars, and the office of single judge.

BERTRAM F. GRIFFIN, JCD
Portland, Oregon

THE LAITY IN THE REVISED CODE

I. *Who are the Laity?*

There are in the Church, by divine institution, sacred ministers, called clerics, and other Christian faithful, called lay persons (204, §1).[1]

Lay persons are:
- configured to Christ by baptism
- strengthened in the faith by confirmation
- participate in the saving mission of the Church
- take on a specific work, especially that of giving witness to Christ in the ordering of temporal matters and secular affairs in accord with God (c. 225).

Lay persons are incorporated into Christ by baptism and, together with all the Christian faithful, constitute the People of God. Consonant with one's proper canonical state of life, each, in one's own way, participates in the priestly, prophetic and kingly works of Christ. Thus, all the Christian faithful are called to exercise the mission which God entrusted His Church to fulfill in the world (c. 204).

II. *The Revised Code uses the term "Christian Faithful." Who are they?*

The revised Code directs itself to those of the Christian faithful who are in full communion with the Catholic Church on earth, viz.,
- the baptized joined with Christ in visible fellowship
- by the bonds of profession of faith, sacraments, ecclesiastical government (c. 205).[2]

---

[1]From both of these groups, there are Christian faithful who by vow or other bond, recognized and ratified by the Chruch, profess the evangelical counsels and are consecrated in a special way to God (these persons are commonly known as "religious" - c. 207, §2).

[2]Catechumens, in a special way, are a part of the Christian faithful, joined with the Church and enjoying special prerogatives proper to Christians (c. 206).

Unless otherwise stated in the Code those persons are not bound directly by merely ecclesiastical ordinances who have not yet accepted the Gospel and have not been baptized, and those baptized non-Catholics in Churches and communities separated from the Catholic Church, even though the former are related to the Church in various ways and the latter are joined in a certain, even if not perfect, communion with the Catholic Church (c. 11).

These persons, incorporated into the Church of Christ by Baptism, are at the same time constituted persons with all the duties and rights proper to a Christian (c. 96).

III. *What are these duties and rights proper to all the Christian Faithful?*

All of the Christian faithful enjoy a true equality in dignity and action, and, according to one's proper state in life and work, are to cooperate in the building up of the body of Christ (c. 208).

All the Christian faithful:

- ought to lead a holy life, promoting the Church's growth and one's own sanctification (c. 210);
- have the duty and right to work together that the divine plan of salvation may touch more effectively all persons at all times everywhere (c. 211);
- are bound, conscious of one's own responsibility, to follow in obedience the teachings and rulings of the bishops (c. 212, §1);
- are free to make known to their pastors their wishes and needs, especially spiritual ones (c. 212, §2);
- have the right, and sometimes even the duty, according to one's knowledge, competence, and position, to make known to the bishops their opinions on things pertaining to the good of the Church, always showing concern for the integrity of faith and morals, and the common good and dignity of persons (c. 212, §3);
- have the right to worship God according to their own approved rite, and to follow their own form of spiritual life, consonant with Church teachings (c. 214);
- have the liberty to freely found and moderate associations for the purpose of charity or piety (when not reserved by their nature to Church authority) or for fostering the Christian vocation in the world; and to hold meetings for these purposes (cc. 215; 298-329);
- have the right to share in the Church's mission and to initiate on their own projects for promoting and sustaining apostolic activity (c. 215);
- have the right to a Christian education, the knowledge of the mystery of salvation, and instruction in right living, appropriate to one's maturation (cc. 217; 229);
- have the right to choose a state of life, free from all coercion (c. 219);
- have the right to a good reputation which no one may illegitimately harm; (c. 220);
- have the right not to be punished by canonical penalties, except according to the norm of the law (c. 221, §3);

- have the right to vindicate and defend their rights in a competent ecclesiastical forum according to the norm of the law, (c. 221, §1);
- have the right of appeal and the right to be judged by the prescriptions of the law applied with equity (c. 221, §2);
- have the duty to provide for the needs of the Church so that what is needed for divine worship, apostolic works, charity and a just sustenance for its ministers will be provided (c. 222);
- can exercise their rights individually or in associations, taking into account the common good of the Church, the rights of others, and one's duties toward others (cc. 223; 298-329).

Particular reference is made to:

- parents, who especially have the most serious duty and right to educate their children and to teach them according to the doctrine of the Church (c. 226, §2);
- students of the sacred sciences, who enjoy a freedom of inquiry, with due compliance to the magisterium of the Church; indeed, they should prudently declare themselves in those matters in which they are competent (c. 218).

A final canon in this section in the Code notes that the ecclesiastical authority is competent to moderate for the common good of all the above rights or to restrict them by invalidating or incapacitating laws (c. 223, §2).

IV. *Are there specific duties and rights proper to the Lay Christian Faithful?*

Lay persons have the duty and right, individually or in associations, to work that the divine message of salvation may be made known and accepted by all persons everywhere in the world. This duty is all the more urgent in situations where people can hear the Gospel and know Christ only through lay persons (c. 225, §2).

Lay persons are to be acknowledged as possessing the right to civil liberty; however, in exercising that right, they should take care that their actions are imbued with the spirit of the Gospel and that they direct their attention to the magisterial teaching of the Church, sincerely avoiding proposing their own opinions as Church teaching in debatable matters (c. 227).

Lay persons who are married have, by reason of matrimony and the family, a vocation and an office to work for the building up of the People of God. Moreover, they have a right to pastoral and canonical assistance in this area from the pastors of the Church (c. 226, §1).

Lay persons who qualify can be called by bishops to ecclesiastical offices and works, in accord with the law, and those who are outstanding in due knowledge, prudence and honesty, can assist bishops as experts and counselors (even in synods, councils, etc.) in accord with the law (c. 228).

Lay persons have the duty and the right to acquire a knowledge of Christian teaching so that in exercising their part in the apostolate they may live it, proclaim it, and, if necessary, defend it. Therefore, they have the right to attend ecclesiastical universities and schools of religious studies and to receive academic degrees. Those who qualify, in accord with the law, can receive the mission to teach the sacred sciences from legitimate ecclesiastical authority (c. 229).

Lay men who qualify can be instituted permanently to the ministries of lector and acolyte (however, this does not confer on them the right to sustenance or remuneration from the Church) (c. 230, §1).

All lay persons can be deputized temporarily to serve in the office of lector, and all enjoy the faculty of serving in the offices of commentator, cantor, and others, according to the norm of the law (c. 230, §2).

Lay persons, in cases of need when there are no sacred ministers, can supply for these offices by ministering the Word, presiding at liturgical prayer, conferring baptism and distributing Communion (c. 230, §3).

Lay persons who permanently or temporarily give themselves to a special service of the Church are obliged to be properly formed for this work, and they have a right to a fitting and proportionate remuneration to provide for themselves and their families, and, to the extent that it can be provided, social security and health insurance (c. 231).

V. *How does all of this actually affect the lay person?*

The revised Code offers:

- a more detailed and extensive treatment of the duties and rights of the lay person (cc. 204; 205; 207; 224-231);
- less discrimination; all the baptized constitute the People of God, and, while there are obviously diverse offices and duties, all are equal in dignity and common action by reason of baptism (cc. 204-205; 207; 208);
- a special emphasis on the common priesthood of the faithful with the lay person participating more actively in the Eucharist and offering his or her priestly ministry in sacramental actions, prayer, thanksgiving, charity and witness of a holy life (cc. 204; 205; 208; 210-216; 225; 327-329);
- more extensive involvement on the part of the lay person, including the holding of an ecclesiastical office and cooperating in the exercise of the power of governance (cc. 124-145), e.g., as a judge in a collegiate tribunal (c. 1421, §2);
- more consultative involvement, e.g., as delegates at diocesan synods (cc. 460-468), members of the diocesan pastoral council or a parish council[3] (cc. 511-514; 536), parish leadership roles and on-going pastoral leadership positions for ongoing pastoral care (c. 517).[4]

---

[3]These are not mandatory institutes but are to be instituted if pastoral solicitude recommends it.
[4]A priest directs these activities since only a priest can be a pastor of a parish (c. 521, §1).

Lay persons now can:

- exercise an increased number of non-ordained ministries, where needed, e.g.
    - chancellor (c. 483)
    - notary (c. 483)
    - procurator-advocate (c. 1483)
    - promoter of justice (c. 1435)
    - defender of the bond (c. 1435)
    - judge (c. 1421, §2)
    - diocesan business managers (c. 494)
    - members of diocesan or parish finance councils (cc. 492-494; 537)
    - represent the person of the Holy See as members of Pontifical Missions or as members of heads of delegations to international councils, conferences or congresses (c. 301) acolytes[5]
    - lectors[6] (cc. 230; 910, §2)
    - extraordinary ministers of the Eucharist
    - deputized extraordinary ministers of exposition of the Blessed Sacrament (c. 943)
- preach[7] (c. 766)
- receive the canonical mission to teach theology and other sacred sciences (c. 229, §3)
- be missionaries (c. 784)
- be catechists (c. 785)
- be assigned to act as extraordinary ministers of baptism (c. 861, §2)
- be delegated to assist at weddings (c. 1112).[8]
- administer Sacramentals (1122).

The revised Code stresses the role of the family and its vocation in building up the Church (c. 226, §1). Parents are the primary educators of their children and have freedom of choice in the selection of schools (c. 793). All others are to assist them in this goal of education.

The revised Code emphasizes the parish as a community of persons (cc. 515-552). Lay persons are called to a more active role (cc. 517, §1; 528). As cited above, they can participate in a wider variety of offices and ministries, some formerly reserved to clerics.

In addition to the contents of these canons, lay persons continue to possess a strong moral power, a strong innovative influence. They continue to maintain

---

[5]Only males may be acolytes (c. 230, §1).

[6]Only males may be permanent lectors (c. 230, §1). Other lay persons can be deputized temporarily to serve in the office of lector (c. 230, §2).

[7]The homily at the Eucharist, however, is reserved to priests and deacons (c. 767, §1).

[8]The bishop may do this with the authorization of the episcopal conference and the Holy See (c. 1112, §1).

the power of receiving or not receiving all of the law or some of the law. Ultimately they still possess the power of numbers, of finances, of public opinion, of *sensus fidelium*, of conscience and the radical power of shaking the dust from their feet as they exit or worse, stay on apathetically.

RICHARD G. CUNNINGHAM, JCD
Brighton, Massachusetts

THE RIGHTS AND OBLIGATIONS OF CLERICS

I. Introduction

The canons which deal with the rights and obligations of the clergy are rooted in the documents of the Second Vatican Council, principally *Lumen gentium*, Chapter III, *Christus Dominus*, Chapter II, and *Presbyterorum ordinis*, the entire document. Although Chapter III of Book II deals with the rights and obligations of clerics as clerics, there are rights and obligations which are applicable to clerics in virtue of their office as pastors and associate pastors (Book II, Chapter IX, which should be discussed under the same title). In any case, the above-mentioned documents together with the early *motu proprios*, most notably *Ecclesiae Sanctae*, should be restudied before beginning a commentary on these canons.

The Code accepts the basic conciliar definition of the Church as "the People of God" and legislates Church mission and ministry within the context of a hierarchical communion (*Lumen gentium*, Chapt. III, n. 18).

Although the Code emphasizes the authority of clergy, particularly bishops and presbyters, they are directed to honor the charisma of lay persons and invite their collaboration in the work of Church ministry (cc. 129; 275, §2; 517, §2; 529, §1; 1421, §2).

The Church of Vatican II is clearly reflected in the Code. Yet in many respects the pastoral practice of the Church has progressed beyond the notions espoused at the Council. Any commentary on the new Code, therefore, will be inadequate without theological reflection on present pastoral practice since the close of the Second Vatican Council. While it is true the Code has solidified certain definitions and structures and determined the rights and roles of certain persons in the Church, the Code nevertheless leaves room for the application of recent insights into the mission and ministry of the Church. An example of this may be seen in canon 528, §1 in which pastors are encouraged to become involved in the promotion of social justice. It is hardly more than an honorable mention. Nevertheless, it is becoming clear from the recent practice of the American bishops, the work of social justice plays a major role in the life of the pastoral leader. This factor has created a significant increase in literature and commentary on the appropriate role of the clergy in social issues. This issue also touches upon the degree to which a priest may become involved in politics (cc. 285, §2, §3; 287, §2).

Institutions, codes and systems are established to help people become more than they could become without those institutions. When systems cripple people psychologically or spiritually, they must be evaluated and, if necessary, changed so that the members of the institution can freely commit themselves to its ideals and goals. Church processes, systems and institutions are not ends in themselves. They are intended to enable people to move toward wholeness and salvation.

People are the most valuable resource of any institution. Priests, in particular, are a most valuable, indeed, an essential resource within the Church. Decisions made at the diocesan level should encourage and foster the growth of the presbyterate as much as the growth of the people of God within the diocesan church.

Priests possess the same basic human needs as those of lay persons — physical security, a sense of belonging, self-esteem and a share in determining their destiny. Institutions are challenged today to provide an environment in which these basic human needs can be addressed.

At the same time, it must be recognized that these needs cannot be fully met this side of the parousia. Moreover, concentration on self to the exclusion of others can only lead to selfism and disillusionment. Yet, it must be admitted that people do mature when they take serious responsibility for their life and actions. When a person has little or no control over his life, he remains immature and tends to treat others in a like manner, exceptions notwithstanding.

The Church should be in the vanguard in promoting that spiritual freedom which enables its members to offer a total "yes" to God in imitation of His Son, who was obedient to the Father in all things, even death itself. It is a holy paradox that those who have the greatest potential for obedience to the will of God are those who are most spiritually free, aided, of course, by divine grace. The Code then, can only set minimal standards which govern and guide the external behavior of its members, especially the clergy.

In the Rite of Ordination of Priests, the ordaining bishop reminds candidates for the priesthood and the faithful assembly that "presbyters are co-workers of the college of bishops since they are joined to bishops in the priestly office and are called to serve the people of God."

As principal pastor of the diocesan church, the bishop has a primary concern for all the people of God entrusted to him. His position is not one of honor, but of service. It is his sensitive responsibility to discern with his brother priests how their gifts and charisms can be used most effectively in meeting the pastoral needs of that portion of the people of God called the diocesan church. His love for his brother priests can be no less than his love for all the people. They are his "partners in the ministry of Christ" (Rite of Ordination for Bishops). Therefore, it is his challenge to collaborate with them in such a way that they, too, will mature in their love for God and neighbor. "I must distinguish carefully," says St. Augustine, "between two aspects of the role the Lord has given me, a role that demands a rigorous accountability, a role based on the Lord's greatness rather than on my own merit. The first aspect is that I am a Christian; the second, that I am a leader for your sake; the fact that I am a Christian is to my own advantage, but I am a leader for your advantage . . . as a leader I must give Him [God] an account of my stewardship."

The instruction contained in the Rite of Ordination concludes with a plea to work in union and harmony with the bishop and try to bring the faithful together like a unified family so that they may be led effectively through Christ and in the Holy Spirit to God the Father. The clergy are urged to remember the example of the good shepherd who came to serve rather than be served.

Although the new Code may only move the Church officially from a Vatican I to a Vatican II definition of the Church, it does not deny the dynamism that must be part of a living organism.

Consequently, the prudent practitioner of the law will be a wise counselor who is able to bring out of the Code both new things and old, which honor the tradition and recognize the power of the Spirit guiding the growth and development of the Church into the future.

II. RIGHTS AND OBLIGATIONS OF CLERGY

A. *Rights of Priests*
1. Only the clergy can assume offices which require the power of orders (c. 274).

Although the law allows deacons and lay persons to participate in pastoral ministry due to the shortage of priests (c. 517, §2), only a priest can be appointed to the full pastoral care of souls (c. 150).

The revised Code also gives stability to the office of pastor. His appointment is for an indefinite period of time. (c. 522).

2. Right to join with others in the pursuit of goals that conform to the priestly state (c. 278, §1).

3. Right to an adequate income in remuneration for the fulfillment of their priestly ministry. This income should be commensurate with their position, adequate for their necessities and sufficient for the priest to give an equitable income to those whose services he may require in the fulfillment of his responsibilities (c. 281, §1).

4. Right to social assistance which will provide for their necessities in time of illness, incapacity, or old age (c. 281, §2).

5. Right to a reasonable period of vacation (c. 283, §2).

Pastors and associate pastors are entitled to one month's vacation (cc. 533, §2; 550, §3).

B. *General Obligations for Clergy*
1. Unless legitimately prevented, priests are bound to assume and faithfully fulfill the assignment given to them by their ordinary (c. 274, §2).

2. May not be absent from the diocese for a notable period of time without at least the presumed permission of one's own ordinary (c. 283, §1).

3. Bound by a special obligation to reverence and obedience to the Holy Father and to his own ordinary (c. 273).

4. As consecrated in a special way to God and as dispensers of God's mysteries in the service of the people of God, priests are obliged to seek spiritual perfection in their own lives (c. 276, §1).

5. Bound to daily recitation of the Divine Office (c. 276 §2, 3°).

6. Obligated to undertake spiritual retreats in accord with local regulations (c. 276, §2, 4°).

7. Bound to celibacy (c. 277, §1).

8. Act prudently in their habitual association with persons when such association can endanger celibacy or cause scandal (c. 277, §2).

9. Avoid groups or associations whose goals and activities are not in conformity with clerical obligations or interfere with the fulfillment of their priestly responsibilities (c. 278, §3).

10. Continue sacred studies, follow the solid teaching based on scripture, handed down in tradition, accepted by the Church and set forth especially in documents of the councils and popes, avoiding innovations based on worldly novelty and false knowledge (c. 279, §1).

11. In accordance with local law, participate in continuing education courses and conferences with the aim of acquiring a greater knowledge of the theological sciences and pastoral methods necessary to fulfill priestly responsibilities (c. 279, §2).

12. Wear suitable ecclesiastical attire in accord with norms of the episcopal conference and local custom (c. 284).

13. Completely avoid whatever is unbecoming to their state of life in accord with local norms (c. 285, §1).

14. Avoid those things which, though not unbecoming in themselves, are inconsistent with the priestly state (c. 285, §2).

15. Forbidden to assume public office, especially one which involves the exercise of civil power, without permission of both the proper bishop and the bishop of the place where he intends to exercise administrative authority (c. 285, §3).

16. Without permission of the bishop, priests may not undertake the administration of property which belongs to lay persons or to assume a secular office which requires the duty of rendering an account; also forbidden to offer bail even upon security of his own property without consulting the ordinary. Priests are also forbidden to sign a surety for an obligation to pay money (c. 285, §4).

17. Forbidden, without permission of legitimate ecclesiastical authority, to conduct business or trade either personally or through others, for personal gain or for the benefit of others (c. 286).

18. May not take an active role in political factions or in the management of labor unions unless, in the judgment of the competent ecclesiastical authority and with its permission, it would be required for the protection of the rights of the Church and for the common good (c. 287, §2).

19. May not enter military service without permission of the bishop (c. 289, §1).

20. Priests are to take advantage of civil laws exempting them from duties and public offices foreign to the clerical state (c. 289, §2).

21. As cooperators with the bishop, priests have the duty to proclaim the gospel of God (c. 757).

22. Priests must regard preaching as a priority inasmuch as their primary responsibility is the proclamation of the gospel to everyone (c. 762).

23. Priests must see to it with zeal that they stir up and teach the Christian faith, especially through the ministry of the Word (c. 836).

24. Priests have the obligation to give the sacraments to the faithful who are properly disposed and are not prohibited by law from receiving them (c. 843, §1).

25. Priests are obliged to give the sacraments only to Catholics and are forbidden to give them to non-Catholics except in circumstances permitted in the law (c. 844, §1).

26. Permanent deacons are not bound by the requirements of canons 284, 285, §§3 and 4, 286, 287, §2 (i.e., numbers 12, 15, 16, 17, 18 above).

C. Responsibilities of Pastors

1. Pastor is bound by the obligation of providing that the Word of God be proclaimed integrally to all in the parish. This is emphasized in several canons as a primary duty not of pastors but of all priests with the care of souls (cc. 528, §1; 702).

2. As part of the duty of announcing the Word of God, the pastor must see to it that the faithful are taught the truths of the faith (c. 528, §1).

3. One of the chief obligations the pastor has in teaching the truths of the faith is to see to it that homilies are given at least on Sundays and days of precept (cc. 528, §1; 767, §4).

4. The pastor has a grave duty to provide catechetical instruction to all of the people committed to his care. This catechesis is to be provided for adults and in a special way to children and the young. In this important responsibility, the pastor is to utilize the resources of other priests, religious, laity (cc. 528, §1; 773, 776; 777).

5. Pastor must also strive with every effort to bring the gospel message to the faithful who may have fallen away from belief in a practice of the faith (cc. 528, §1; 771, §1).

6. Pastor also should be solicitous of bringing the evangelical message to non-believers in his parish (cc. 528, §1; 771, §2).

7. Pastors have the duty of making available the means whereby all the faithful may receive a Catholic education (cc. 528, §1; 794, §2).

8. Pastor must also support activities in which the spirit of the gospel and what concerns social justice are promoted (c. 528, §1).

9. Paraphrasing Vatican II, the revised Code calls on the pastor to make the Eucharist the center of the life of the parish, especially through frequent recep-

tion of Communion and penance, through family prayer, through participation in the Sacred Liturgy which he, under the authority of the bishop, should regulate and ensure that no abuses occur (c. 528, §1).

10. Again borrowing from the Vatican II decrees as well as from the 1917 Code, the revised Code urges the pastor to know his people, visit their homes, share in their concerns, anxieties and especially in their grief at the time of death, comforting them; in time of failure, correcting them prudently; assisting the sick, especially those near death; solicitously comforting them with the sacraments and commending their souls to God (c. 529 §1).

11. It is the duty of the pastor to acknowledge and support the proper role which the laity have in the mission of the Church, promoting their associations which have religious purposes (c. 529, §2).

12. Pastor must cooperate with the bishop and the diocesan presbyterate in striving to achieve parish community. He must bring the people to the point where they see themselves also as members of the diocese and of the universal Church (c. 529, §2).

13. As in the present law, the revised Code lists certain functions of the pastor. While in the 1917 Code it calls them functions reserved to the pastor, the revised Code is more realistic and describes them as functions entrusted to the pastor. They are the following (c. 530):

a. Administration of baptism. In the 1917 Code, solemn baptism is reserved to the pastor.

b. Administration of confirmation to the dying. This faculty is not in the 1917 Code though pastors have had this faculty for many years.

c. Administration of Viaticum, anointing of sick, imparting of apostolic blessing. In the 1917 Code, it is carrying Viaticum that is reserved. Similarly reserved in the 1917 Code is carrying the Eucharist publicly to the sick. This reserved function was repeated in the schema of the new Code but removed in the final revision of October, 1981.

d. Assist at marriages and impart the nuptial blessing. Omitted in the revised Code is the reserved function of announcing the banns for ordinations and marriages.

e. Perform funeral services.

f. Bless the baptismal font at Holy Saturday services, leading processions outside the church, giving solemn blessings outside the church.

g. More solemn celebration of Eucharist on Sundays and days of precept. This function is new and is not in the 1917 Code. Omitted in the new Code is the 1917 Code's reserved function of blessing homes on Holy Saturday.

14. In all juridical transactions, the pastor acts in the name of the parish. He must take care, therefore, that he administer the property of the Church in accord with canonical norms (c. 532).

15. Pastor is obliged to reside in a parish house near the church. Bishop can permit him to reside elsewhere, especially in a residence with other priests, provided he can still carry out his parochial functions adequately (c. 533, §1).

16. Pastor is obliged to offer the *Missa pro populo* for his parish on Sundays and days of precept. If impeded, he is to do so on other days or through some other priest (c. 534, §1). In the 1917 Code, the number of Masses was about 88. Over the years, the list was simplified until the norm of the revised Code which limits the obligation to Sundays and days of precept.

17. The pastor has the responsibility of providing and assiduously maintaining parish registers for baptism, marriage, and the dead. While the schema also called for a confirmation register, this requirement was eliminated in the final revision of October, 1981 and it is now left to local law to determine if necessary (c. 535, §1).

18. The pastor must also see to it that all required annotations be placed in the baptismal register (c. 535, §2).

19. Pastor must keep a parochial seal (c. 535, §3).

20. Pastor must maintain archives in which are to be kept the parish registers as well as letters from the bishop and other important documents (c. 535, §4).

21. If the bishop judges it useful, the pastor must establish a parish pastoral council over which he presides (c. 536, §1).

22. Pastor must have a parish finance council utilizing the laity to help in the administration of parish property (c. 537).

23. Pastor, in accord with diocesan norms, should at regular intervals hold retreats or missions or other spiritual exercises adapted to the needs of the parish (c. 770).

24. Pastor has responsibility to keep custody of the holy oils obtained from the bishop (c. 847, §2).

25. Pastor has a special obligation concerning the sacrament of matrimony. He is obliged to see to it that his ecclesial community gives support to the faithful so that the marital state is maintained in the Christian spirit and grows toward perfection. The Code then suggests some methods that he could utilize to achieve this important goal (c. 1063).

D. *Responsibilities of Associate Pastors*

There are very few canons on the rights and obligations of associate pastors, referred to in the Code as "parochial vicars." Inasmuch as they are collaborators of the pastor, with few exceptions what applies to pastors also applies to associate pastors.

1. When appointed the associate pastor becomes the cooperator with the pastor in the pastoral care of the parish but under his authority (c. 545, §1).

2. The details of obligations of the associate pastor are left to diocesan regulations, the letter of appointment by the bishop, and especially to the instructions given to the associate by the pastor (cc. 548, §1; 545, §1).

3. The associate pastor is obliged to assist the pastor in carrying out the pastoral ministry to the whole parish, excluding the application of the *Missa pro populo*. When circumstances warrant it, the associate pastor takes the place of the pastor (c. 548, §2).

E. *Exhortations*
1. Since all priests are working together to achieve the same goal, the building up of the Body of Christ, they should be united among themselves in a bond of fraternity and prayer and should strive for cooperation with each other in accord with local law (c. 275, §1).
2. Priests should recognize and promote the mission which the laity exercise in the Church and in the world (c. 275, §2).
3. Among the means priests may utilize in striving for spiritual perfection in their own lives, the following are recommended:
    a. Faithfully and zealously fulfilling their pastoral ministry;
    b. Reading of scripture;
    c. Reception of the Eucharist; especially urged is daily celebration of Mass;
    d. Meditation;
    e. Frequent confession;
    f. Devotion to the Blessed Virgin Mary;
    g. Other means of sanctification (c. 276, §2).
4. Especially valuable for priests are those societies or associations which afford a fraternal support, encourage holiness in the priestly ministry and promote fraternal unity among priests and with the bishop (c. 278, §2).
5. Should study even non-sacred sciences especially those related to the sacred sciences, particularly if they help in the pastoral ministry (c. 279, §3).
6. Strongly recommended is some form of community life for priests. Where it exists, it should be maintained (c. 280).
7. Priests should cultivate a simplicity of life and shun anything that smacks of worldliness (c. 282, §1).
8. Exhorts priests to give any surplus funds they may have after providing for their own necessities, to the activities of the Church and to charitable causes (c. 282, §2).
9. Should promote as much as possible the preservation of peace and harmony among all people (c. 287, §1).

III. SELECT BIBLIOGRAPHY

Bishop A.J. Bevilacqua. "Priestly Life and Ministry." Pittsburgh Seminar on the Revised Code (March, 1982).
Dutch Bishops. Closing Statement of the Special Dutch Synod, Rome, January 31, 1980. *Origins* 9/35 (1980).
P. Murnion. "Ministry That is Specifically Ecclesial." Address to National Catholic Vocation Council, August 12, 1979. *Origins* 9/13 (1979).

P. Murnion. "The Unmet Challenges of Vatican II." Address to Catholic Theological Society of America, Cincinnati, 1981. *Origins* 11/10 (1981).

Pontifical Council on the Laity. "Identity and Mission of Priests Within Associations of the Laity." Study document. *Origins* 11/34 (1982).

Pope John Paul II. Address to Priests of Rio de Janeiro, 1980. *Origins* 10/9 (1980).

Pope John Paul II. Address to Brazilian Workers, July 3, 1980. *Origins* 10/9 (1980).

Sacred Congregation for the Clergy. "Declaration on Associations of Priests, Politics and Labor." March 2, 1982. *Origins* 11/41 (1982).

J.S. Teixeira. *Personnel Policies: A Canonical Commentary on Selected Current Clergy Personnel Policies in the United States of America*. Canon Law Studies 503. Washington, D.C.: Catholic University of America, 1981.

U.S. Bishops' Committee on Priestly Life and Ministry. "The Priest and Stress." Report. *Origins* 11/42 (1982).

KENNETH E. LASCH, JCD
Paterson, New Jersey

SUBSIDIARITY AND THE CHURCH LAWYER

Subsidiarity is a basic principle in the new Code of Canon Law. As a principle, subsidiarity states that decisions should be taken at the most appropriate level (not necessarily at the lowest level, but the most appropriate level). At the most appropriate level for decision making there must also be a corresponding level of responsibility. The new Code, recognizing the principle of subsidiarity, is a Code for an adult Church, a Church of law, not of personal whim.

We must understand that the Code is not a compilation of statutes. It presupposes custom, legal doctrine and jurisprudence. The new Code is shorter than the 1917 Code of Canon Law (1752 canons as opposed to 2414 canons). Much in the new Code is left to episcopal conferences, regional or plenary councils, and diocesan synods.

Now that the Code is promulgated, its reception is going to depend on commentaries and popular teaching as well as on the method of implementaiton. The Church lawyer in the future is going to be called upon to assist in preparing appropriate legislation for the episcopal conference as well as for diocesan synods and regional or provincial councils. We must be careful not to jump too fast into the area of legislation and be patient with the need to develop consensus and general overall policies, before too swift implementation.

Particular law is going to be more and more important. In the Vatican II Church, particular law has many forms of expression: legislation in the strict sense, hopefully not too excessive, as well as practical guidelines, directories, constitutions, or statutes for Church consultative bodies, and policies hammered out on the diocesan level outside the synod. The Church lawyer must truly be a *Church* lawyer in the future and not merely a "canon" lawyer.

BERTRAM F. GRIFFIN, JCD
Portland, Oregon

NATIONAL CHURCH STRUCTURES

The Episcopal Conference

The revised Code devotes thirteen canons to the episcopal conference. This conference has a major role in the local church as a clearing house for ideas and policies. The episcopal conference is a planning institute on a national level for pastoral activity and the apostolate. Hence, the episcopal conference will exercise a lot of its role in terms of pastoral coordination, the publication of directories, the development of consensus and the undertaking of regional projects.

Still, there are many explicit references to the episcopal conference's influence on the local level in terms of particular law. The following is not meant to be a complete list of all the specific references to the episcopal conference and the new law, but like the catalogues in *Finnegan's Wake*, can give a feeling for the extent of the episcopal conference's influence in Church life.

Regarding ministry

The episcopal conference establishes norms for the formation and training of permanent deacons (canon 236) and norms for the training of priests and for the *Ratio Studiorum* (canon 242).

The episcopal conference can erect a national seminary with the approval of the Holy See and approve its statutes (canon 237, §2).

The episcopal conference can establish norms on clerical dress (canon 284).

The episcopal conference establishes the age and qualifications for the installed ministries of lector and acolyte (canon 230). Parenthetically, these ministries — as in the document *Ministeria Quaedam* — are still restricted to men.

Regarding the diocese

The episcopal conference establishes norms and provides for the pension of retired bishops (canon 402, §2) and norms for the pensions of pastors (canon 538, §3).

The episcopal conference can establish norms for the council of presbyters (canon 496).

The episcopal conference can permit term of office for pastors (canon 522).

The episcopal conference can establish norms for parish records over and above those for baptism, marriage, and the deceased (canon 535, §1).

Regarding the teaching office
The conference can establish norms for promoting participation in the ecumenical movement (canon 755, §2);

Norms for the reception of penance, Eucharist and the anointing of the sick by baptized non-Catholics in cases of necessity (canon 844);

Norms for lay preaching (canon 766), for radio and TV preaching (canon 772, §2);

Norms for religious education in schools and on the radio or TV (canon 775);

Norms for participation of clerics and religious in radio and TV programs regarding Catholic doctrine and morality (canon 831, §2).

With the approval of the Holy See the episcopal conference may publish a national catechism (canon 775) and set up a national catechetical office to assist dioceses in the region.

The episcopal conference establishes norms for the ordering of the catechumenate and determines the rights and obligations of catechumens (canon 788). Interestingly enough, in number 14 of the Decree on Missionary Activity *Ad gentes*, Vatican II states: "The juridical status of catechumens should be clearly defined in the new Code of Canon Law." The new Code, on the principle of subsidiarity, relegates the juridical status of catechumens to the episcopal conference, apparently on the assumption that the rights and obligations of catechumens and their status in the Church will differ from continent to continent and nation to nation.

Finally, the episcopal conference should be responsible for the distribution of universities and Catholic faculties (canon 809), and higher institutions of religious studies (canon 821).

Regarding the liturgy
The episcopal conference can issue norms in regard to sacramental ministry in an ecumenical context, namely, sacraments of penance, Eucharist, and anointing of the sick for non-Catholics in danger of death or other grave need (canon 844, §4).

The episcopal conference also has extensive influence over the catechumenate, as mentioned above. The conference sees to preparation of vernacular translations of liturgical books (canon 838, §3); can adapt the *Ordo Initiationis* (canon 851), and issue special liturgical norms in this area. Again, as an interesting sidelight, the new Code suggests that fourteen year olds and older should be referred to the bishop for baptism. This represents a European bias where there are very few non-baptized people. In Italy, for example, if you are non-baptized, you are either Jewish or belong to a very deeply ingrained Masonic or Communist family. A restriction was also in the 1917 Code of

Canon Law, but for sixteen year olds. In the United States, all pastors and generally all priests have faculties to baptize adults.

The episcopal conference can issue norms regarding the celebration of the sacrament of baptism by infusion and immersion (canon 854).

Although the normal age for confirmation is the age of discretion, the episcopal conference can establish a different age (canon 891).

The episcopal conference can establish norms for the confessional and attached grill (canon 964).

The episcopal conference has extensive influence in the area of marriage preparation. It can establish norms regarding the pre-nuptial inquiries and the banns (canon 1067). The age for valid celebration of marriage is fourteen for girls and sixteen for boys in the new Code. The episcopal conference can establish a higher age for the licit celebration of marriage (canon 1083) although it cannot establish an invalidating impediment. The episcopal conference can establish norms for the ritual of marriage (canon 1120), for the registration of marriage (canon 1121), and for the mixed marriage promises (canon 1126).

In the revised Code of Canon Law the holy days of obligation are retained, but the episcopal conference can abolish or transfer some of them to the nearest Sunday (canon 1246, §2).

The episcopal conference can also establish additional rules on abstinence or provide for the substitution of other kinds of works (canons 1251 and 1253).

Regarding other matters

For *financial matters* the conference establishes norms for support of the Church (canon 1262), norms for other fund raising events (canon 1265), social security for the clergy not provided by civil society, norms for leasing Church property. The episcopal conference also establishes a maximum and minimum sum for the alienation of stable patrimony (canon 1292). In *tribunal matters* the episcopal conference may permit a single judge in first instance (canon 1425), may set up regional appeal courts (canon 1439), and can require every diocese to set up a conciliation office or panel (due process) (canon 1733).

The Plenary Council

The episcopal conference is not basically a legislative body. Legislation on the national level or its equivalent is done by plenary council. The episcopal conference has legislative power only on two occasions: when canon law prescribes it (for example, the conference must decide whether to convoke a plenary council); and secondly, when mandated by the Holy See. The Holy See may mandate such legislative activity at the request of the conference, or the Holy See itself may take the initiative. Legislation enacted by the conference must be passed by a 2/3 majority of the membership in these cases; otherwise, if the episcopal conference wishes to pass legislation in cases other than the two above, unanimous consent is required.

The plenary council is a council of all the particular churches in the territory (i.e., dioceses). The episcopal conference decides on the frequency of the plenary council, convokes it, selects a site, sets the agenda, and opens and closes the council. The members of the plenary council are the same as the episcopal conference; other members can, and some must, be invited with consultative vote, including both priests and lay people (canon 443). The decisions of the plenary council bind the local bishop. For special pastoral reasons, as is always the case in Church law, the local bishop can dispense from appropriate decrees in his own diocese.

NATIONAL PASTORAL COUNCIL

In the revised Code there is no consultative pastoral council on the national level. National consultations (like *Call to Action*) are, of course, always possible. Each nation and the episcopal conference must find its own way on the principle of subsidiarity.

SUMMARY

There are several advantages to the new approach of the revised Canon Law toward subsidiarity. The episcopal conference and plenary council can establish laws and policies at the local level. In this way, law can be adapted to local needs much more easily then under the former Code. The episcopal conference has a responsibility to proceed with such legislation but with care and discernment. The Code should not be seen as a complete recipe book for church order; the episcopal conference, therefore, should be judicious in legislating for the particular church and understand the need for subsidiarity on that level as well. The making of law on the regional level, however, also has the advantage of the ability to change law more rapidly than on the universal level. There is certainly a greater possibility for involvement of the ecclesiastical community in the formation of national policy and law both through formal intervention and certainly and above all through informal consultation.

There are some disadvantages to this process of law-making on the regional level. There is first of all the American danger of over-legislating. Americans seem to find it hard to leave matters to discretion and interpretation. It would be, in my opinion, very dangerous for the episcopal conference to begin legislating minute details that really should be left to provincial or diocesan law, just as it is dangerous for provincial or diocesan law to legislate matters that should be left to the discretion and interpretation of pastors. Secondly, we all recognize that the episcopal conference meets once or twice a year, and that it takes a long time for the episcopal conference to come to a decision. At times this may be viewed as a disadvantage, at times as an advantage and corrective to the American tendency to over-legislate. Finally, at the present time we have no clear way of promulgating and collecting regional law. The episcopal conference should develop a national church law digest or gazette where the decisions of the episcopal conference can be communicated in a clear and well-defined manner.

BERTRAM F. GRIFFIN, JCD
Portland, Oregon

DIOCESAN CHURCH STRUCTURES

Diocesan Synod

Nine canons deal with the diocesan synod which is the legislative body on the diocesan level. True, the bishop remains the sole legislator in the diocese, but the synod is a powerful consultative body whose purpose is to assist the bishop in legislating for the particular church the common pastoral good. In the original draft, the synod was scheduled to be held at regular intervals, every ten or at most twenty years. At the latest review this was removed, and the synod is now held at the discretion of the bishop in consultation with the presbyteral council.

The synod is composed of the auxiliary bishop and episcopal vicars, members of the presbyteral council, laity to be selected by the pastoral council, the urban and rural vicars and one presbyter from each area or vicariate, the seminary rector and religious superiors located in the diocese; even observers from the non-Catholic community may be invited.

The laws of the synod which the bishop accepts are to be forwarded to the metropolitan and the episcopal conference; they do not require the approval of the Holy See or even have to be sent there.

Diocesan Consultative Bodies

Five consultative bodies are part of the post-conciliar Church. Two are obligatory: the presbyteral council (with the college of consultors), and the finance council (or administrative council). Two are optional though recommended: the diocesan pastoral council, and the episcopal council or bishop's cabinet. One is not mentioned in the revised Code: the coordinating council of the apostolate, recommended by the Second Vatican Council (Decree on the Apostolate of the Laity, *Apostolicam actuositatem*, no. 26).

1. *The Presbyteral Council and College of Consultors*
The presbyteral council is required in every diocese. It is composed of the presbyters or priests of the diocese and is the "senate" of the bishop, representing the presbyterium. The statutes of the presbyteral council are approved by

the bishop in accordance with norms set up by the episcopal conference. The statutes should determine the membership of the council; approximately one-half are to be elected by the presbyters themselves. Ex officio members are permitted as well as others named by the bishop as he so desires.

Those who have active and passive vote in the presbyteral council are all incardinated secular priests as well as secular externs and priests from religious institutes and societies who reside in the diocese and exercise an office for the good of the diocese. Particular law and statutes might also permit other resident priests such as members of religious orders without diocesan offices. The statutes should determine the manner of election; the diverse regions and ministries of the diocese should be represented.

The bishop convokes the council, presides over it, and sets a portion of the agenda by determining questions to be treated; members of the council can determine other agenda, but the bishop is free in receiving proposals for discussion and recommendation.

It seems that a five year term of office is presumed, although the actual term is to be determined in the statutes. When the see is vacant, the presbyteral council ceases and the college of consultors takes over. The bishop can dissolve the presbyteral council after consulting the metropolitan, but he must reinstitute the council within a year.

The diocesan consultors are to be six to twelve priests appointed by the bishop from among the members of the presbyteral council. The consultors have a five year term, or if a consultor ceases as an elected member of the presbyteral council because of a shorter term of office he should be reappointed to the council as a bishop's appointee or serve as an ex officio member for the remainder of his term of office as consultor.

The college of consultors has two basic functions in the revised Code.

First, the college acts as a governing board when the see is vacant. The presbyteral council ceases and the consultors remain. The new bishop submits his Apostolic Letters to the consultors and the chancellor. The consultors elect the administrator for the diocese who may not remove the chancellor or other notaries without consent of the consultors. The college of consultors also acts as a governing body of last resort when the see is impeded (through captivity, exile, or inability of the bishop to communicate with his diocese). Finally, the coadjutor bishop must also submit his letters of appointment to the consultors and the chancellor.

Secondly, the college of consultors acts as financial trustees of the diocese together with the finance council. The college of consultors must be consulted regarding the nomination and removal of the business manager, and both the college of consultors and the finance council must give their consent for extraordinary acts of administration and for the alienation of stable patrimony of the diocese within limits set by the episcopal conference.

Although the presbyteral council is consultative only, the bishop is required to consult with the council of presbyters on several occasions, and the members of the council of presbyters (as mentioned above) have the right and obligation to participate in the diocesan synod and advise the bishop on legislation for the diocese.

The presbyters must be consulted whenever the bishop wants to erect, suppress, or make a notable change in parishes (canon 515). They must be consulted regarding the remuneration of priests who help in parishes when they are not pastor or associate pastor in that parish (canon 531). The bishop may establish pastoral councils in every parish after consulting the presbyteral council (canon 536). The bishop must consult the presbyteral council before imposing assessments on parishes (canon 1263).

2. Personnel Boards

Although personnel boards are not in the revised Code, the concept of consultation is part and parcel of the new law. According to the new law, the council of presbyters and the bishop select a board of pastors which is somewhat equivalent to a combination of the present parish priest consultors and diocesan examiners. The bishop must consult at least two pastors from this board in the removal of impaired pastors (canon 1742) and in the transfer of pastors against their will to another parish or office (canon 1750). Moreover, the Code instructs the bishop to consult the area vicar before appointing a pastor to a vacant parish within that vicariate (canon 524), and suggests that the bishop might well consult the presbyters and people. The bishop also is advised to consult the pastor and area vicar regarding the appointment of an associate pastor (canon 547).

Other elements of interest to personnel boards include the following.

The definition of an impaired pastor (canon 1741) includes behavior which causes grave harm or disturbance to the ecclesial community: incompetence, lack of skill, mental or physical infirmity which prevent the pastor from fulfilling his role, loss of reputation or aversion on the part of serious and dedicated parishoners, serious neglect or violation of pastoral duties even after a warning, bad financial management (unless other means can be used to correct this problem), or any other behavior which causes the pastor's ministry to be harmful or inefficacious.

The episcopal conference can grant a decree permitting diocesan bishops to appoint a pastor for a definite term (canon 522).

Team pastorate is now in universal law. The pastoral care of a parish or parishes can be entrusted in solidum to a team of priests. The entire team is pastor; one member is moderator who directs the common action and is accountable to the bishop (canon 517, §1).

The new universal law also permits lay exercise of pastoral care. Because of a lack of priests, the bishop can entrust a parish to a deacon, a lay person, or a lay and religious pastoral team, providing a neighboring priest acts as pastor and moderator (canon 517, §2).

Several neighboring parishes can be entrusted to one pastor because of lack of priests or for other reasons. Hence, there is no absolute need to reduce parishes to missions, to consolidate or close them merely because they lack a resident pastor (canon 526).

Pastors are requested to retire at the age of seventy-five (canon 538, §3).

3. *Diocesan Finance Council*

The revised Code requires every diocese to have a diocesan finance council, or a council on administration. The diocesan bishop or his delegate presides over this council which is composed of at least three members of the faithful (clergy or lay) qualified in financial matters and in civil law, and appointed by the bishop to a five-year renewable term of office. The finance council approves the annual financial statement of the diocese and prepares the annual budget in accord with the direction of the bishop.

The finance council must be consulted in several areas. The bishop, for example, may impose an assessment only after consulting with the presbyteral council and the finance council (canon 1263).

The bishop must consult the finance council for major administrative acts and must have its consent as well as the consent of the college of consultors for extraordinary acts as defined in universal law and the constitutional by-laws of the finance council (canon 1277).

The bishop consults the finance council in determining the extraordinary administrative acts of pastors (canon 1281).

Pastors and other administrators must make annual financial reports to the ordinary, who presents them to the finance council for the council's consideration; reports are also made to the faithful in keeping with the directives of the particular law (canon 1287).

Bishops and pastors need the consent of the finance council and the college of consultors to alienate portions of the stable patrimony of the Church in amounts determined by the episcopal conference (canon 1292).

The ordinary needs to consult the finance council prior to investing in trusts and foundations (canon 1305).

The ordinary needs to consult the finance council prior to reducing requirements of foundations (canon 1305).

4. *Consultation*

The fact the presbyteral council and finance council are only consultative even though they are mandatory, should not discourage advocates of shared responsibility. Consultation in the revised Code is not a mere pro forma act. Canon 127 states that if consultation is required by law, the majority of the group to be consulted must be consulted for the validity of the administrative act, unless particular law provides otherwise. If consent is required by law, it must be obtained for validity. Moreover, the administrator (bishop or pastor) should not act against the advice of consultors, especially if they are concordant, unless he has a prevailing reason. Hence, the Code clearly recommends consensus management as a decision making style and process in the Church, allowing for discretion on the part of the bishop or pastor, but recommending that a consensus be achieved and that the administrator follow the consultation of appropriate bodies.

5. *Diocesan Pastoral Council*

The diocesan pastoral council is recommended both in the revised Code and in the *Directory on the Pastoral Ministry of Bishops*. The pastoral council is basically a planning organization. It investigates, evaluates, and proposes practical conclusions regarding the pastoral activity in the diocese. It is composed of Catholics, members of the clergy, religious institutes, and especially lay persons representing various regions, social conditions, professions, and apostolates in the diocese. The pastoral council meets at stated times under the direction of the bishop and ceases when the see is vacant. It is consultative only and the bishop presides over the council and must convoke it at least once a year.

6. *Episcopal Council*

Another recommended agency on the diocesan level is the bishop's cabinet or episcopal council. The vicars general and episcopal vicars of the diocese form the episcopal council. One of the vicars general is appointed moderator of the chancery staff and his work is to coordinate the work of the curia and supervise the work of other staff members. All auxiliary bishops are also vicars general or vicars episcopal. The diocesan chancellor now is no longer required to be a priest. The chancellor in the 1917 Code as well as in the revised Code is basically an office manager.

In the American Church the office of chancellor, through delegation, became equivalent to vicar general. Whether the American Church adopts the more traditional language and method of organization remains to be seen.

The episcopal vicars represent the bishop either in districts of the diocese, or with special groups such as language groups, or special ministries of the Church.

The Code does not mention other offices such as superintendents of schools or Catholic charity directors. These two could obviously be included in the bishop's cabinet, if he so desires. The bishop's curia does have two support offices: the business manager who has a five-year contract, and the office manager or chancellor who may be a priest or a lay person.

7. *Coordinating Council for the Lay Apostolate*

The Second Vatican Council's Decree on the Apostolate of the Laity recommends that councils be set up on the diocesan and parish level to coordinate the various lay associations and undertakings, recognizing their particular nature and autonomy (AA 26). The coordinating council is not mentioned in the *Directory on the Pastoral Ministry of Bishops*, although both documents urge coordination of the lay apostolate on the diocesan, vicariate, and parish levels, by means of staff meetings, forums, and other group or intergroup relationships.

Canon 394 recommends that bishops promote and coordinate the works of the apostolate, preserving their proper nature or autonomy. This coordination should be done on a diocesan or at least regional level. A council for this purpose is not included in the revised Code.

Area vicars have as their first office, to promote and coordinate common pastoral action in the area (canon 555).

The absence of the coordinating council for the apostolate in the revised Code does not mean that such a coordinating council is not a possible option for both the diocesan and parish level. As a matter of fact, on the parish level in this country, this particular passage from the Decree on the Apostolate of the Laity (AA 26) is used as the Vatican II justification for the parish council. Unfortunately in many dioceses, the diocesan pastoral council is viewed as basically a coordinating council in the style of the paragraph of the Decree on the Apostolate of the Laity rather than as a planning council as described in *Christus Dominus* (CD 27).

OTHER STRUCTURES

It might be useful to point out other examples of Vatican II structures not mentioned in the revised Code. Again let me add that their omission does not mean they are forbidden, but merely that they are now left to particular law and local option on the basis of the principle of subsidiarity.

1. *The Liturgical Commission*

This commission is mandated in the Constitution on the Sacred Liturgy (SC 45 and 46) along with a coordinated commission on sacred music and sacred art. The Instruction on the Proper Implementation of the Sacred Liturgy in 1964 and the Instruction on Music of 1967 repeat this norm. Interestingly enough, the *Directory on the Pastoral Ministry of Bishops*, like the revised Code of Canon Law, omits reference to liturgy commissions, sacred art commissions, or sacred music commissions.

2. *Catechetical Organization*

The *General Catechetical Directory* published by the Sacred Congregation for the Clergy discusses the organization for catechesis on the diocesan level and proposes structures whose purposes are to promote catechetical activities and to cooperate with other apostolic undertakings and works (for example, with the liturgy commission, associations for the lay apostolate, the ecumenical commission, etc.). The *Directory* does demand that every diocese have a catechetical office which is staffed and it refers, on the parish level, to such structures as the parish catechetical center and the Confraternity of Christian Doctrine. The board of education, educational commission, etc., are not mentioned in the revised Code.

3. The Ecumenical Commission

The *Directory Concerning Ecumenical Matters*, part 1, published in 1967, recommends a diocesan ecumenical commission. This commission is not mentioned in the revised Code or in the *Directory on the Pastoral Ministry of Bishops*.

4. Commission for New Parishes

The *Directory on the Pastoral Ministry of Bishops* does suggest a diocesan commission for new parishes which works in consultation with the priests' council and other concerned commissions. This particular diocesan commission is not repeated in the revised Code.

COORDINATION

The American Church since the Second Vatican Council has attempted to develop structures for shared responsibility. Unfortunately, we have often used political and business analogies. Hopefully the revised Code will provide us with an opportunity to return to a more ecclesiologically founded form of church government. Our greatest temptation is to create hierarchical collegiality with extensive organizational charts showing how every organization, commission, apostolate in the diocese is coordinated by a super-board. The revised Code of Canon Law suggests the importance of coordination, but does not demand that this be done by a super-board or coordinating council. The pastoral council is basically a planning council. Coordination might well occur through such agencies as the episcopal council or bishop's cabinet. In any event, the super-board which has delegates from all the other diocesan commissions has not demonstrated its effectiveness in the American Church on the diocesan level. The concept of such a super-board still persists, however, on the parish level, and perhaps needs to be challenged.

Political analogies are still being quoted in articles on church organization.

At one time, planners and amateur structural experts conceived of church government on the English model with the episcopal conference representing the House of Lords and the national pastoral council representing the House of Commons. The concept of a national pastoral council or parliament was considered not feasible several years ago. On the diocesan level, however, the presbyteral council is sometimes still viewed as a House of Lords and the pastoral council as the House of Commons — with the bishop as King George!

Some dioceses try to solve the problem of coordination on the French political model. The presbyteral council, the sisters' council, and a lay council organized with parallel authority are imagined analogously to the three Estates. Each of these councils sends delegates to a diocesan pastoral council viewed as an Estates General. The bishop alternates between the Sun King, trying to dissolve the pastoral council, and Louis XVI, being dissolved by it.

A friend of mine who studied in Rome suggests that the diocesan structure is really taken from Roman Law where the presbyteral council is the *Senatus* and the pastoral council is the *PopulusQue Romanus*. The bishop in this model comes out as Caesar or Imperator.

Another friend of mine who did not have the benefit of studying in Rome suggests that the bishop and his presbyters are basically analogous to King John and the Barons. The sections on rights and freedoms, and on due process in the revised Code of Canon Law are the Magna Carta and the Second Varican Council is Runnymeade.

The revised Code, although adopting Montesquieu's division of powers into legislative, judicial and administrative or executive, maintains nevertheless the tradition of the bishop as the sole legislator, sharing his legislative authority on a consultative basis with the diocesan synod and, to a lesser degree, with the presbyteral council. Diocesan financial administration is shared with the finance manager and the finance council. Judicial authority is exercised by the tribunal. The planning process occurs through the diocesan pastoral council and coordination of pastoral action is viewed on the diocesan level as a staff function of the episcopal vicars and, outside the chancery, as a coordinating function of the urban and rural vicars.

TRIBUNALS AND PASTORAL PLANNING

Without going into detail on the complex issue of procedural law, several elements of the revised Code could be of interest to pastoral planners.

1. *Staffing*
The single judge permitted by the American Procedural Norms is retained in the new law with permission of the episcopal conference. The single judge must be a priest. The defender of the bond and the auditor may now be lay persons. The procurator, the attorney, and the notary — as at present — may be lay persons. The judge must at least have a J.C.L.; the defender of the bond must also have a licentiate in canon law.

2. *Appeal Process*
The appeal process must be conducted by a three-judge tribunal. At least one of the judges may be lay. An additional defender of the bond, who may also be lay, is required at the appeal level. All of these persons must have a licentiate in canon law. All cases must now be reviewed. The possibility of dispensation from review and appeal has been removed from the revised Code.

3. *Regional Tribunals*
Because of the additional personnel and the tremendous case load of local tribunals, I suspect that regional tribunals will be established in the United

States. These are now provided for in the new law under the episcopal conference.

4. Defect of Form

Defect of form cases must now be handled in summary process with a citation of the other party and a decision. The former law permitted mere consultation with the ordinary.

5. Privilege Cases

The pauline privilege and the so-called petrine privilege are retained basically as at present. Norms for privilege cases involving one baptized person are not given in the Code but are governed by directives from the congregation for the Doctrine of the Faith.

The effect of the revised Code is going to demand the education of lay professionals and some financial outlay on the part of the Church. Hopefully, American ingenuity can provide word processors, computers, and other examples of technology to minimize the otherwise extravagant demand on both staff and money for vindicating and defending one's rights and freedoms.

THE PARISH

In the revised Code the parish is defined as a stable community of the faithful within a particular church whose pastoral care is committed to a priest as the proper pastor under the authority of the diocesan bishop.

As a general rule, parishes are territorial. However, personal parishes may also be set up within a given territory with membership based on rite, language, national origin, etc. Hence, in the new law, multiple or cumulative membership in several parishes is even more possible than under the present rather restricted notion of territoriality.

The pastor's ministry is a ministry of teaching, sanctifying, and governing or pastoring with the cooperation of other presbyters and deacons and in consultation with the laity.

The pastor has a finance council or council on administration; this is obligatory. The council itself has consultative vote and assists the pastor in the administration of the parish (canons 537 and 532).

The diocesan bishop may establish a policy that every parish also have a pastoral council, and in doing so he must consult the presbyteral council. The pastoral council is to include the pastor, members of the parish staff and members of the parish. The purpose is to promote pastoral action. The council has consultative vote (canon 536).

Coordination of parish organizations and apostolates is not mentioned in the revised Code nor does it mention how the finance council and the pastoral council relate. The American enthusiasm with hierarchical collegiality and super-boards has produced the "parish council," which performs all the functions of pastoral planning, administration, and coordination not only of the ministries of the parish, but often of all parish organizations and apostolates. This concept, of course, is not forbidden by the new law; but the law wisely suggests, in my opinion, that pastoral planning, administration and coordination of what we in this country call ministry (but which in the law is called the apostolate) might well be separate structural problems. With the introduction of the new law, the people in parish council ministry will, hopefully, have an opportunity to reflect on our past experience. It may well be that we will see emerging a true pastoral council on the parish level, leaving the development and coordination of ministerial committees and apostolic lay organizations to parish staff, thereby avoiding the growing sense of boredom on parish super councils where the only action month after month is hearing reports from committees, commissions and organizations, each having a reserved seat on the board.

Bertram F. Griffin, JCD
Portland, Oregon

CONSULTATION WITH INDIVIDUALS OR GROUPS
REGARDING EPISCOPAL DISCRETION

Prenote: Canon 127, §2, 2° requires the bishop to consult in order to act validly in various diocesan undertakings. [Where *consent* and not only consultation is required, will be indicated below.]

A. *Council of Priests* (cf. c. 500 on general rules re: consultative role)

1. 461, §1: decision of bishop re: advisability of diocesan synod; no set time for synod.

2. 515, §2: modification of parishes; i.e., erection, modification, division, suppression (cf. also c. 813 permitting bishop to set up university parish to meet pastoral needs of students; nothing explicit re: council of priests).

3. 531: determination of use of offerings of faithful on occasion of parish services; to be placed in general parish fund.

4. 536: decision re: appropriateness of parish councils and structuring of guidelines for such councils.

5. 1251, §2: decision regarding permission to build a church (also to be consulted: rectors of neighboring churches).

6. 1222, §2: decision to permit church to be converted to secular purposes for reasons other than its poor condition. (*Consent* of those with vested rights is also required.)

7. 1263: decision regarding imposition of diocesan tax for needs of diocese on public juridical persons subject to bishop; also, extraordinary and moderate tax for very grave needs to be imposed on other juridical persons and on physical persons (finance council also to be consulted). [New canon, not in 1917 Code, approved at October, 1981 Code Commission meeting.]

8. 1742, §1: choice of stable corps of pastors from persons proposed by bishop to be available for processes of transfer or removal of pastors.

B. *College of Consultors* (c. 502: between 6 and 12 priests chosed by bishop from council of priests)

1. 272: must consent before administrator can permit excardination, incardination or migration of clergy after see is vacant for one year.

2. 485: consent for administrator to remove chancellor or other notaries.

3. 494: hiring and firing of fiscal manager; finance council also to be consulted.

4. 501, §2: *sede vacante* fulfills role of council of priests.

5. 413, §2: choice of administrator in *sede impedita* situation if no other provision made.

6. 419: governance of diocese initially *sede vacante* provided no other arrangements made.

7. 421, §1: election of administrator with 8 days of vacancy.

8. 422: college to notify Holy See of vacancy.

9. 1277: bishop to obtain their consent for acts of extraordinary administration (along with consent of finance council).

10. 1292, §1: consent (with consent of finance council) to alienate diocesan property.

C. *Pastor-Consultors*

1. 1742, §1: preliminary discussion of possible removal of pastor with two pastors from group chosen by priests' council.

2. 1745, 20: discussion of pastor's objections to removal with bishop.

3. 1750: discussion of pastor's objections to transfer with bishop.

D. *Dean*

1. 524: consultation re: appointment of pastor. (Other priests and laity *may* be consulted.)

2. 547: possible consultation re: appointment of parochial vicar [associate pastor]. (No explicit reference to consultation when parochial vicar is removed —cf. c. 552.) Pastor himself may be consulted re: appointment of parochial vicar.

E. *Finance Council*

Cf. c. 492, §1: a group of at least 3 experts in financial affairs and civil law, presided over by bishop or his delegate; laity or clergy without any distinctions [Original schema provided for at least 1 member of priests' council to be a member of this group, but this was not retained as a requirement in the promulgated Code.]

1. 493: to prepare annual budget according to bishop's determination and to submit annual financial report at end of fiscal year.

2. 494, §§1 & 2: hiring and firing of fiscal manager (along with college of consultors).

3. 494, §3: setting guidelines for functioning of fiscal manager.

4. 494, §4: fiscal manager to submit financial report to council. (537: no specific reference to finance council; but perhaps it should be consulted before bishop draws up guidelines for parish finance councils mandated in revised law.)

6. 423, §2: finance council to choose fiscal manager *sede vacante*, if fiscal manager elected diocesan administrator.

7. 1263: episcopal decision to impose taxes on physical or juridical persons (cf. no. 7 under council of priests, above on "A" list).

8. 1277: bishop to hear finance council in significant administrative issues; bishop needs their consent regarding acts of extraordinary administration (along with consent of college of consultors).

9. 1281, §2: episcopal determination of acts of extraordinary administration for institutes subject to his control if statutes do not specify this.

10. 1287, §1: examination of annual (financial) report of non-exempt administrators in the diocese.

11. 1292, §1: consent required for episcopal authorization of alienation within minimal and maximal sums determined by episcopal conference (also with consent of college of consultors, and of interested parties).

12. 1305: episcopal authorization to place money and mobile goods in a safe place and to invest them (interested parties also to be heard).

13. 1310, §2: episcopal reduction of burdens imposed in executing last wills for pious causes, if such burdens cannot be fulfilled (interested parties also to be heard).

Note: There is no explicit obligation for the bishop to consult the finance council in the following areas, but such consultation might well be in order. This is not to say that only the finance council need be consulted.

1. 1265, §1: permission of ordinary necessary for physical or juridical persons to collect money.

2. 1266: possible authorization of special collection to be taken up in all churches for various ecclesial undertakings.

3. 1274, §3: bishop to use common fund in diocese for various ecclesial needs.

4. 1276: ordinary to be vigilant re: administration of goods in public juridical persons subject to him; he is to issue appropriate guidelines.

5. 1281, §1: episcopal authorization of acts of extraordinary administration by subordinate administrators.

6. 1284, §2, 6°: episcopal consent necessary for investment of excess capital by subordinate administrators.

7. 1288: episcopal authorization for subordinate administrators to engage in civil litigation (cf. 1301-1302 for variance on execution of wills).

THOMAS J. GREEN, JCD
Washington, D.C.

PRESBYTERAL COUNCILS

1. Generally, the canons continue the law which has been in force since the Second Vatican Council when presbyteral councils were authorized. The revised Code should not require any substantial changes in practice.
2. The purpose of the presbyteral council is clearly set forth in canon 495:
   a. It is a body of priests. Only priests are mentioned as belonging, no reference is made to include deacons.
   b. It is to serve as the senate of the bishop. In the 1917 Code, this term is used for the cathedral chapter or, in this country, for the board of consultors. Clearly the presbyteral council is to be the senate, the preeminent consultative body among priests.
   c. The scope of the council's concern is quite broad—all those things which pertain to the pastoral welfare of the diocese.
   d. The focus of the council's role is primarily in terms of governance. Governance in the revised Code relates to the "munus regendi"—legislative, executive and judicial. While the council is consultative and not judicial or legislative, it has a concern for all those areas in a consultative manner.
3. The council is to have its own statutes. It is not subject to whim or fancy, whether by individuals on the council or diocesan authorities. Once the statutes have been drawn up, taking into consideration the law and any norms which the N.C.C.B. may issue, they are to be approved by the bishop and then observed for the future.

Clearly, the revised Code expects the statutes to specify a number of practical details. For example, canons in this section call for the statutes to deal with how many members are elected (about one half; the statutes can specify more), how many are ex officio; they can extend the right to vote and to run for office to priests living in the diocese who are not incardinated there or doing special service for the diocese; they determine how the elections are to be run and the term of office for members.

The statutes may cover other matters as well. The constitutions of most senates already provide for a number of practical details and will continue in force under the revised Code.

4. The revised Code will require some adjustments in those dioceses where priests incardinated in the diocese may vote but, if they are outside the

diocese, may not run for office. This, I think, is a minor detail and was recognized as such by the Code Commission. In the normal course of events, a priest who is outside the diocese would not be able to attend meetings unless special provision were made for this.

5. One of the changes introduced in the wording of the revised Code relates to the bishop's relationship to the council. Canon 500, §1 may be interpreted as requiring a more direct involvement of the bishop in the ordinary operations of the council — calling meetings, setting agenda, chairing the sessions. I think this would be misreading the canonical tradition that underlies this canon.

The council is not to meet without the bishop's authorization; but the actual notifications of meeting, etc., do not have to be done by the bishop. Similarly, the sessions do not have to be chaired by the bishop; he can — and, for the sake of achieving the purpose of the council as a place of dialogue, reflection and counsel, probably should — preside but let someone else chair the meeting itself. The same provision has been in effect relative to diocesan pastoral councils from the very beginning and the system of someone else chairing the meetings has proven feasible and profitable.

The Circular Letter of the S. Congregation for the Clergy on Presbyteral Councils (October 10, 1969) spoke about the bishop proposing items to the council or freely accepting issues raised by the members. The wording in the canon continues this position. This does not exclude other priests in the diocese from proposing items for the agenda; it does mean that the council retains control of its agenda, so that either a council member or the bishop himself would have to actually place the item on the agenda. It does not mean, however, that council members can deal only with items proposed by the bishop. Rather, the bishop is free to accept or not accept proposals the council has developed on its own initiative.

6. There are some cases in the revised Code where the bishop must listen to the presbyteral council. These include whether to hold a diocesan synod; to set norms about stole fees and about the support of those who do parochial ministry, whether full- or part-time. The bishop must consult the council on various pastoral matters: to erect, suppress, or make innovations in regard to parishes; to mandate parish councils in every parish; to give permission to build a church building or to permit an existing church building to be converted to profane use; to impose a diocesan assessment (other than the seminary tax).

7. The procedure for the removal of pastors has been revised. In this procedure the bishop must make use of two pastors drawn from a panel set up by the presbyteral council. That is, the bishop proposes a list of pastors to the council; the council selects those who will form an ongoing panel; when troubles arise, the bishop must draw on those approved by the council to form this panel, as part of the consultative process in removing a pastor.

8. The relationship of the presbyteral council to the college of consultors has raised some problems in the past. The revised Code attempts to resolve these in two ways. First, members of the college of consultors must be selected

from among the members of the presbyteral council. As consultors they have their own term; but they may continue as members of the council. Indeed, there is nothing to prevent the statutes of the presbyteral council from keeping the members of the college of consultors on the council for the duration of their five-year term as consultors.

This approach has attempted to retain the freedom of the bishop to select advisors for certain key matters, but to continue the close tie of consultors with the preeminent clerical consultative body, the council. It may prove difficult in dioceses with very small councils; e.g., if the council has only fourteen members, the bishop will have to de-select two in order to meet the limitation of twelve members for the college of consultors. However, it is always possible to seek an indult to raise the limit within reason, and experience may point to other solutions to this problem.

The second way the revised Code attempts to resolve the consultors-council issue is by limiting the issues the consultors may deal with. Canon 502, §1 indicates they are to deal with the matters specified in law. These include the naming and removing of the economus (financial manager) of the diocese, and certain other financial matters. Aside from those matters, the bishop is to consult with the presbyteral council (canon 495, §1) if he wishes to consult with a body of priests.

Moreover, there is nothing to keep the presbyteral council from dealing with financial matters, even though it is not bound to do so, and even though the college of consultors must deal with them. The bishop is not bound to seek the council's advice in these matters, but there is nothing which would seem to prohibit the council from offering its advice.

James H. Provost, JCD
Washington, D.C.

This study was originally done as part of a report to the National Federation of Priests' Councils.

PERSONNEL ISSUES

I. Introduction

In recent years we have witnessed a dramatic increase in the number of lay persons becoming involved in formal Church ministry. Various theories have been proposed to explain this phenomenon. Those of more traditional background suggest the serious shortage of vocations to the priesthood and religious life as the reason why more lay people must become involved. Others of a different pastoral perspective suggest that the phenomenon stems not so much from the shortage of vocations as from a renewed emphasis on the basic baptismal call to Christian service. The discussion has resulted in a debate about who are qualified for Christian ministry and who for Christian service. The discussion is not over, but the new Code clearly recognizes the need for lay persons to participate in the exercise of pastoral ministry in collaboration with a presbyteral or episcopal moderator or overseer. It would seem the intent of the Code to maintain a basic connection between the power of orders and the power of jurisdiction. Therefore, the exercise of formal lay ministry and, to a great extent, the ministry of the deacon, is ordered to those activities which do not require those powers intimately connected with priestly ordination. In practice, deacons and lay persons may certainly be considered collaborators in ministry and even carry out significant pastoral responsibilities in partnership with members of the presbyterate.

As with that section of the Code which deals with the rights and obligations of the clergy, commentators and practitioners should bear in mind that the new Code reflects the doctrine and documentation of the Second Vatican Council, in effect moving the Church from Vatican I to Vatican II. Pastoral practice since the close of Vatican II, coupled with the reflections of theologians, may legitimately influence the interpretation and application of the Code to personnel issues.

Most, if not all, personnel offices are still directed toward the distribution of clergy personnel, including in many dioceses, permanent deacons. Some personnel offices have begun to function as clearing houses for lay persons seeking a pastoral position within a parish or other pastoral institution. However, the appointment of non-clerical persons is not a canonical appointment nor does it carry with it any official canonical title, e.g., pastor, associate pastor.

Some dioceses have accepted a title such as "parish minister" or "pastoral associate." Although commissioning ceremonies have been designed to solemnize the appointment of parish ministers to pastoral staffs, such ceremonies are not assumed to have canonical force. Nevertheless, the justice and the basic rights of Church members must be recognized and safeguarded in the employment practices and policies governing lay ministry.

Latest reports indicate that the number of priests can be expected to decline over the next two decades. It will become increasingly necessary to promote lay ministries and new pastoral structures through which the Church will be able to continue her mission. The Code has at least opened the door toward a more creative approach to pastoral ministry. Several dioceses are already well on the way toward a more holistic approach to collaborative pastoral ministry without dishonoring the norms prescribed in the new Code.

II. SELECTED PERSONNEL ISSUES

A. *The Appointment of Pastors and Associate Pastors*

1. Only a priest can be validly appointed pastor (cc. 521, §1; 517, §1; 150). His appointment should be based on those qualities and virtues necessary for the responsible exercise of his office (cc. 521; 547).

2. The diocesan bishop is the one who freely appoints pastors and associate pastors (cc. 521; 547).

3. In appointing a pastor, the bishop has the obligation of assigning the priest whom he considers suitable in view of all circumstances. Therefore, the bishop is not required to appoint the one subjectively most qualified.

4. In determining the suitability of a candidate, the bishop should seek the advice of the vicar forane, who may conduct an appropriate inquiry. The bishop may also consult other priests and even lay persons (c. 524).

It is under this canon that the role of the personnel director and the personnel board should be discussed. It is clear from the Code that the personnel director and the board are advisory to the bishop, who retains full freedom. However, the bishop may not act arbitrarily nor should he show favoritism. It should be kept in mind that although it is the responsibility of the vicar forane to be solicitous for the welfare of the priests within his vicariate, he must also look to the common good of all the people. The vicar forane is not a vicar for clergy. It must be assumed that the needs of a parish are to be seriously considered in determining the priest most qualified to be appointed pastor.

5. Ordinarily, a pastor should be appointed as the pastor of one parish (c. 526 §1). Moreover, in the same parish there can be only one pastor. In the case of a shortage of priests, one pastor may be appointed pastor of several neighboring parishes. It is important to note that these neighboring parishes retain their identity as parish. They are not reduced to the status of a mission. Moreover, the Code serves to envision the collaboration of lay persons with the pastor.

This canon excludes the appointment of co-pastors to one parish. However, two priests may be appointed to form a team *in solidum*. In this case, one of the team must be appointed "moderator" (c. 517, §1).

6. Term of Appointment. The new Code stresses the stability of the office of pastor. His appointment, therefore, is for an indeterminate period of time (c. 522). All indults to the contrary cease with the promulgation of the code (c. 6, 2°. Episcopal conferences may issue a special decree permitting the bishop to limit the tenure of pastors. The episcopal conference must first seek the confirmation of such a decree from the Holy See in the usual manner (cc. 522; 455, §2).

No mention is made of tenure for parochial vicars (associate pastors). The new Code does state that the bishop may remove or transfer an associate pastor "for a just reason" based on the needs of another parish or on those of the parish to which he is assigned.

The Code does not seem to provide for any rights for associate pastors other than a period of one month vacation and Christian burial. However, the bishop may approve diocesan policies which honor the human need for security and stability with due process in the assignment process. The whole trend of recent documents on the relationship of bishops and priests emphasizes the mutuality of this relationship. The Code envisions the whole presbyterate as primary collaborators in the government of the diocese. Parochial vicars are to the pastor what episcopal vicars are to the bishop of the diocese. Therefore, associates are primarily collaborators with the pastor.

7. Removal of Pastors

a. No one appointed to an office which he holds for an indefinite period of time can be removed except for serious reasons and only by following the procedure described in the law. The same applies for a priest assigned to an office for a specified period in order for him to be removed before termination of that period (c. 193).

Conditions which justify the removal of a pastor include behavior which may cause serious harm to the pastoral community; mental invalidity or permanent physical illness which renders the pastor incapable of carrying out his duties; loss of reputation in the eyes of serious-minded parishioners or hostility toward the pastor which is unlikely to dissipate; serious neglect of pastoral responsibilities which persist in spite of warning; inefficient administration of temporal goods resulting in serious harm to the Church without possibility of resolution (c. 1741).

b. Procedure for Removal (cc. 1740-1747)

1) When the bishop has reason to believe there is sufficient cause for removal, he must confer with two pastors selected from among those approved for this purpose by the presbyteral council.

2) If after consultation with the two pastors the bishop feels that the serious reasons require the removal of the pastor, he will predently ask the pastor to resign within fifteen days.

3) If after two requests the pastor does not submit his resignation or refuses to do so without giving reasons, the bishop is to issue a decree of removal.

4) If the pastor decides to contest the bishop's action, he is permitted to examine the records of the case and respond in writing. After examining the pastor's written response and, if necessary, after a hearing, the bishop is to discuss the matter with the same two pastors. After this deliberation, the bishop is to decide whether to remove him or not.

5) Once the decree of removal has been issued, the pastor must vacate the parish. If the pastor is ill, the bishop should allow him to remain on the premises for as long as necessary.

6) The pastor still has recourse to the Holy See against the bishop's decision.

7) During this appeal, the bishop may not appoint another pastor but may appoint an administrator.

Comment: The process for the removal of a pastor is administrative, not judicial. Although a last-resort measure, it is not intended to be punitive. Although the consultation with the two pastors is required, the bishop is not bound to follow their counsel, though he would be imprudent to disregard it without serious reason. The bishop must still provide for the sustenance of the pastor by giving him another assignment or by directly providing an adequate income.

8. Transfer of Pastors

a. Transfer looks more to the good of the parish to which the pastor is to be transferred rather than the welfare of the parish from which he is being transferred. The Code offers two reasons to justify a transfer: (1) the good of souls and (2) the necessity or utility of the Church. In fact, any worthwhile reason would justify refusal on the part of the pastor (c. 190, §2).

b. Procedure for Transfer (cc. 1748-1752)

1) Bishop proposes the transfer in writing.

2) If pastor refuses, he should give his reasons in writing.

3) If the bishop's decision remains firm, he should follow the same procedure as that outlined for the removal of a pastor.

9. Retirement. A pastor is urged but not absolutely obliged to submit his resignation upon completion of his 75th year. The bishop will then decide whether to accept or defer the resignation (c. 538, §3). Retirement policies adopted by several dioceses in the United States will need to be re-evaluated in light of this new legislation. If a bishop wishes to impose retirement on an unwilling pastor, he must follow the procedure for the removal of a pastor. It may also be opportune to review the use of the term "retirement." Although a priest may retire from an office, he does not really retire from priesthood. Much more discussion is needed in this area.

10. Residence. Pastors and associates are obliged to reside in a parish house near the church. The bishop can permit residence elsewhere provided they can

still carry out their parochial functions adequately (c. 533, §1). The Code strongly recommends residence for several priests (c. 550, §1).

B. *Team Ministry*

The Code recognizes a new entity called "team ministry" (c. 517, §1).

1. When circumstances require it, the pastoral care of one parish or even of several parishes simultaneously can be entrusted to several priests acting as a team, *in solidum.*

2. One of the priests on the team is to be appointed "moderator" of pastoral care with the responsibility of coordinating joint activities of the team and be accountable for the team to the bishop (c. 517, §1).

The moderator is an episcopal appointment.

The Code makes no mention of anyone except priests as members of the team. The Code, however, does recognize other "parish ministers" or "pastoral associates" as collaborators with priest members. In practice they certainly may collaborate in the exercise of pastoral ministry in those areas for which priestly ordination is not required. Parish ministers or pastoral associates are not to be considered canonical appointments. They may be considered members of the pastoral staff.

3. More than one parish can be entrusted at the same time to the same team ministry group (c. 526, §1).

4. Team members and the moderator enjoy permanent stability and, therefore, are appointed for an indefinite period (c. 542, 2°; cf. c. 522). Therefore, all members of the team share the same responsibilities as pastors.

5. Removal or transfer of the moderator or team members must honor the requirements for removal or transfer of pastors (c. 544; cf. c. 1740-1752).

6. In legal action, only the moderator acts in the name of the parish or parishes entrusted to the team (c. 543, §2, 3°).

7. If one of the priest members or the moderator withdraws or if one of them becomes incapable of exercising the pastoral ministry, it does not result in the vacancy of the parish or parishes (c. 544). The bishop shall appoint another moderator should he withdraw, etc. Until the appointment of a new moderator, the senior priest assumes the role of moderator.

8. All team members are bound by the obligation of residence (cc. 543, §2, 1°; 533, §1; 550, §1).

III. Select Bibliography

Archbishop Joseph Bernardin. "Reflections on the Ministerial Priesthood." *Origins* 11/5 (1981).

Bishop Anthony J. Bevilacqua. "Priestly Life and Ministry." Pittsburgh Seminar on the Revised Code (March 1982).

Suzanne Elsesser. "Full-time Lay Ministers in the Church." *Origins* 10/10 (1980).

Pope John Paul II. "Address to Priests of Zaire." *Origins* 10/1 (1980).

Bishop Francis Quinn. "A Bishop's Vision for Priests." Address to priests of Sacramento, April 1, 1982. *Origins* 12/5 (1982).

J. Stanley Teixeira. *Personnel Policies: A Canonical Commentary on Selected Current Clergy Personnel Policies in the United States of America.* Canon Law Studies 503. Washington, D.C.: Catholic University of America, 1981.

Archbishop Rembert Weakland, O.S.B. "Sharing Gifts and Responsibilities." Address to National Assembly of Women Religious, Milwaukee, August 7, 1980. *Origins* 10/12 (1980).

KENNETH E. LASCH, JCD
Paterson, New Jersey

THE PASTOR'S ROLE
AND SOME IMPLICATIONS FOR SEMINARS

I. MINISTRY OF THE WORD

The first obligation of the pastor is the ministry of the Word, (passing on our tradition). The pastor does this principally

1. by preaching a homily every Sunday and on holy days of obligation
2. by his responsibility for catechetic instruction in the parish
3. by encouraging programs which promote the Gospel spirit, especially regarding social justice.

The pastor has a special responsibility for the Catholic education of the children and young people in his parish.

With the help of other members of the congregation, the pastor is responsible for evangelization of those who have not yet heard the Good News or of the unchurched and those who are no longer active in the Church (canon 528, §1).

It is the proper duty of presbyters, who are cooperators with the bishops, to announce the Good News. Pastors and others who have the care of souls are particularly responsible for announcing the Good News to their congregations or communities (canon 757).

Although presbyters and deacons (unless their faculty is restricted by the local ordinary or unless particular law requires permission) have the faculty from universal law to preach everywhere, the pastor presides over the pulpit, and presbyters and deacons must at least have his presumed permission before they preach in the parish church (canon 764).

The pastor presides over the pulpit and over preaching in the parish church. He is to preach, or to see that a sermon is preached on every Sunday and on holy days of obligation. He may not omit the homily without a serious reason. It is recommended that homilies also be preached at daily Mass, particularly during Advent and Lent, or on the occasion of a funeral or a special celebration (canon 767).

The pastor should also arrange for other forms of preaching, spiritual exercises, missions and retreats (canon 770).

The pastor is responsible for the members of his congregation who rarely, if ever, are able to hear the Word of God. He should see that they receive appropriate instruction. He is also responsible for evangelization of the non-believers in his parish (canon 771, §1).

The pastor has a particularly serious obligation and responsibility for the catechetical instruction of his people (canon 773).

By reason of his office, the pastor is responsible for the catechetical formation of adults, young people and children in his parish. In exercising this responsibility he should enlist the aid of other clerics, religious, and members of the laity, especially catechists (canon 776).

It is the special responsibility of the pastor to oversee
1. general sacramental catechesis
2. the preparation of children for first Communion and first reception of the sacrament of reconciliation
3. for the Sunday School and the extension of catechetical instruction of children who have already made their first Communion
4. for catechetical instruction of the handicapped
5. for the catechetical instruction of adults, both apologetics and enrichment of the Christian life (canon 777).

Since the pastor is responsible for evangelization, canons which refer to the obligations of missionaries are also applicable to the pastor. For example, in evangelization the pastor should make use of catechists, that is, lay members of the congregation or the diocese who are educated and trained for this role and who, under the pastor's moderation, direct the catechumenate (canon 785).

Implications

If preaching, catechetics, and evangelization are the principal responsibilities of the pastor, then the diocese has a right to expect that our seminarians complete their course of studies with a firm grasp of Scripture and of tradition, and an understanding of the principles and methods by which the tradition is passed on in homiletics, catechetics and evangelization. We do not expect our seminarians to be research scholars, although some may be asked to go on for further studies. All of our seminarians, however, should be well trained in Scripture, systematic theology, moral theology, the social teaching of the Church, church history and church structures, and be competent to pass on the Gospel and our tradition in the pulpit, the classroom, and the pastor's study.

II. Liturgical Leadership

The second basic responsibility of the pastor is liturgical presidency.

It is the pastor's responsibility to see that the liturgy in his parish is celebrated in accordance with Church norms, and that the active participation of the laity in the liturgy is promoted. The pastor should see that the Eucharist is the center of the congregational life of the parish. It is his responsibility to see that the faithful are devout in their reception of the Eucharist and the sacrament of reconciliation. The pastor promotes a spirit of prayer in the parish and in the families of the parish (canon 528).

Pastors are responsible for seeing that the faithful are sufficiently evangelized and catechized before reception of the sacraments (canon 843, §2).

Initiation. The pastor presides over the sacraments of initiation; celebration of the sacrament of baptism is reserved for the pastor or those to whom he delegates his office. It is the pastor who is responsible for administration of confirmation in danger of death, and it is the pastor who presides over the blessing of the baptismal font.

Although the deacon and other presbyters are also ordinary ministers of baptism, and when the deacon or presbyter is absent or impeded, a cathechist or another specially delegated lay person can celebrate the sacrament of baptism, nevertheless, it is the pastor who presides over the sacraments (canon 862).

Hence, it is also the pastor who will confirm catechumens after their reception of the sacrament of baptism (canons 883; 866).

It is the pastor's responsibility to see that children who have attained the use of reason are immediately catechised and prepared for the sacrament of first Communion (canon 914).

Sunday Eucharist. It is the pastor who presides over the Eucharist on Sundays and holy days of obligation or at least over the principal liturgical celebration of those days (canon 530, 7°).

Sacrament of Reconciliation. The pastor is responsible for celebrating the sacrament of reconciliation for the faithful and providing opportunities for individual confession on specific days and at specific hours (986).

Marriage. The pastor presides over the celebration of marriage in his parish (canons 530, 4°; 1109).

The pastor should see that the entire congregation provides assistance in promoting the sanctity and stability of marriage, in particular

1. through preaching, appropriate catechesis of young people and adults, the use of the mass media, all of which can instruct the faithful regarding the meaning of Christian marriage and the duties of Christian spouses and parents;
2. personal preparation for entering marriage by which the spouses are prepared for the sanctity and obligations of their new state in life;
3. by a true liturgical celebration of marriage in which it is clear that the spouses represent and participate in the mystery of unity and creative love between Christ and the Chruch;
4. by assistance to married people and through family life ministry for married couples (canon 1063).

Summary and Implications
1. Just as the bishop presides over the liturgy for the particular church, so

the pastor presides over and celebrates the Eucharistic liturgy for the local parish church with the assistance of other liturgical ministers, either temporary or permanent — lectors, acolytes, cantors, extraordinary ministers of the Eucharist, ushers, psalmists, commentators, choirs, etc.

2. And, as the bishop presides over the *Pax*, or the sacrament or reconciliation, for the particular church and entrusts a share of this ministry to the presbyters of his diocese, so in a special way the pastor is responsible for providing opportunities for reception of this sacrament, both in communal celebrations and at stated times during the week.

3. Just as the bishop presides over initiation for the particular church, so the pastor presides over initiation for the local parish church. Deacons and catechists may baptize. It is the pastor who confirms the baptism of those received into the Church after the use of reason. The deacon or catechist might baptize infants, but only under the moderation and supervision of the pastor. The pastor confirms in danger of death. The present law only reserves the confirmation of children baptized Catholics as infants to the bishop. The baptism of young people over the age of fourteen should be referred to the bishop but in this country such baptisms are usually celebrated on the local level under the direction of the pastor.

4. Finally, the pastor presides over the sacrament of marriage with the assistance of catechists and deacons.

Hence, the seminarian should have a firm grasp of sacramental theology and discipline and above all, a clear personal liturgical piety centered on the Eucharist. Unlike religious, who might spend the majority of their life concelebrating, hearing confessions in retreat settings, and never celebrating the sacraments of marriage or initiation, the diocesan priest, being trained for the pastorate, should have a clear understanding of the role of the sacraments in a pastoral setting and be prepared to exercise liturgical pastoral leadership in this area.

III. Pastoral Ministry

The office of pastor includes the responsibility of knowing one's parishioners.

1. Parish visitation is important and puts the pastor in touch with the concerns, the problems, the griefs and the joys of his people, participating with them, comforting them, and intervening as a guide and a counselor when appropriate.
2. The pastor has a special care for the sick, especially those close to death, helping them with his counseling and his prayers and the sacraments.
3. The pastor has a special responsibility for the poor, the afflicted, the lonely, the immigrant, the exile and those with special problems.

4. The pastor has a special responsibility for family ministry, supporting spouses and parents in their duties and way of life (canon 529, §1).

Implication
Hence, the seminarian must be introduced to such pastoral skills and activities as:
1. Pastoral Conversations — whether in the privacy of the church office, in a restaurant over lunch, in the family living room, at someone's bedside in a hospital room, at the place of work. Personal counselling, particularly on issues of religious and personal importance, is one of any pastor's major activities.
2. Pastoral Convening — it is the pastor's initiative which leads him to bring people together in various groups for various purposes, acting as a reconciler, as a group leader, initiating dialogue, playing the role of mediator or arbiter, or merely enabling encounters.
3. The pastor is present in the great creative events of life: childbirth, coming of age, choosing a vocation, marriage. The pastor has to have a sense of celebration of these moments and of the Church's concern for these highly teachable events in people's lives, and the pastor needs skills for dealing with crisis situations where people are suffering, distressed.
4. The pastor is going to need a certain amount of knowledge and technique in the specific area of pastoral counselling.

IV. Enabling Ministry

The pastor should promote the appropriate mission of the laity in the Church and support various lay associations for religious purposes. Moreover, it is up to the pastor to develop a sense of the laity's participation in the mission of the particular church of the diocese and of the works and mission of the universal Church (canon 529, §2).

Pastors should be expected to develop among the laity a sense of shared responsibility and planning for the pastoral action and mission of the parish through parish councils (canon 536).

Throughout the Code there are several references to the development of lay mission and ministry, particulary in the area of catechetics and liturgical ministries.

Implications
Hence, the seminarians should be trained to have a sense of, and the necessary skills to develop shared responsibility, both in government and in ministry on the parish level. The pastor is involved intimately in the lives of

his parishioners. This, however, does not mean that the pastor hugs ministry and decision-making to himself, but, precisely *because* of his intimate involvement in the lives of so many people, he must enable them to take responsibility for the mission and direction of the Church through the many ministries of the local church, both regarding the Church's outreach mission to the world and the Church's ministry to its own members.

V. ADMINISTRATION

Finally, the pastor is the legal representative of the parish and is responsible for the administration of church property and finances (canon 532).

The pastor will be assisted by a finance council or committee made up of lay members of the congregation (canon 537).

Implications

Parish administration was not taught in the seminary prior to Vatican II; priests learned parish administration by oral tradition from their fellow pastors. Certainly parish administration must be taught by the diocese in the new pastor classes which every diocese should begin to initiate. Nevertheless, it does seem that seminaries could give some broad principles and understandings of parish administration, both financial and in terms of personnel management. More and more pastors are going to have to understand job descriptions, charters of accountability, personnel policies, grievance procedures, contracts, as well as balance sheets, budgets, taxes, insurance, security, fund-raising, etc. Admittedly, much of this will be done by lay volunteers, but in very small parishes the pastor cannot avoid certain direct administrative responsibilities. In very large parishes the pastor must have an over-all understanding of parish administration even if he has a staff person with the direct responsibilities for administration itself.

SUMMARY

Hence, the pastor and, therefore, the seminarian preparing for the ministry of pastoring should be trained and skilled in five areas:

1. the area of preaching and teaching, his primary task
2. the area of liturgical celebration, particularly the Eucharist, in a pastoral setting, his co-primary task
3. the area of pastoral care, or counselling
4. the area of Church leadership and enabling shared responsiblity in ministry
5. the area of Church administration.

BERTRAM F. GRIFFIN, JCD
PORTLAND, OREGON

AN OVERVIEW OF *MUTUAE RELATIONES*

Note: The relationship between religious and diocesan bishops is dealt with in several places in the revised Code, especially cc. 673-683 on the apostolate of institutes. However, the revised Code does not fully restate the law on this issue, and a proper understanding of the new Code can be helped by understanding the directives in the 1978 document, Mutuae Relationes. *The following commentary on that document was developed in August, 1978 in response to a request from the ordinary of a diocese in the United States.*

On Pentecost Sunday, May 14, 1978, an important document was promulgated jointly by the Sacred Congregations for Bishops and for Religious and Secular Institutes, bearing the somewhat novel title, "Directive Notes for the Mutual Relations between Bishops and Religious in the Church." It is usually cited by its opening words as *Mutuae relationes (MR)*. While the document can correctly be characterized as significant, it contains little that is new and nothing surprising. It follows logically from the Decree on the Pastoral Office of Bishops, *Christus Dominus (CD)* of Vatican II, nos. 33-35, and from the *moto proprio, Ecclesiae Sanctae (ES)* of 1966, I, nos. 22-40, which implemented *CD* with respect to the relationships between bishops and religious. Essentially, *Mutuae relationes*, inasmuch as it presents legislation or directive norms approved by Paul VI, details procedures and structures for what had already been required by *ES*.

The genesis of the document was a joint Plenary Assembly of the two Congregations in Rome in October, 1975, the 10th anniversary of the conciliar decrees *Christus Dominus* and *Perfectae caritatis*. That assembly addressed three main topics: (1) what bishops expect of religious; (2) what religious expect of bishops; and (3) what are the best means to facilitate successful cooperation between them. At its conclusion it called for a document which would spell out principles and norms (General Introduction, II). *Mutuae relationes* is that document.

MR does not abrogate or amend any legislation in effect in the Latin Church, whether in the 1917 Code itself or in post-conciliar documents (Part II, Introduction). Indeed, it is presented as a continuation and a focus of the process of renewal in the Church sanctioned by the Council (General Introduction, III). There are a number of directives in Part II which are new as normative or obligatory, but which are logical extrapolations of *ES* and of the doctrinal principles of Part I. In many American dioceses the structures man-dated or recommended in Part II have already come into existence.

The purpose of *MR* is to give structure to the relationships between bishops and religious at the diocesan level, as well as at the national and international levels. This is done in order to make such relationships more orderly and stable and thus more beneficial for the Church itself, and to define more clear-ly the respective roles of bishops and religious (General Introduction, III).

MR is divided into two general parts of almost equal length. The first part is entitled, "Some Doctrinal Points," and is intended as a theoretical or systematic theological synthesis of the respective roles or *munera* of bishops and religious, from which principles can be deduced to ground the normative part of the document, "Directives and Norms." This kind of doctrinal or theoretical introduction has been especially characteristic of post-conciliar documents, including the liturgical texts, and has proved welcome and useful in contextualizing and interpreting the dispositive or normative matter. In this document, as in others, it is important to resist the temptation of the pragmatist to turn to the second part immediately. It is especially true of this document that the rules and norms follow logically from the doctrinal premises. Where the norms present problems, as they sometimes do, they are still concrete expressions of the doctrinal introduction.

While the rhetoric of the first part is fully conciliar, its substance is ex-clusively hierarchical. It speaks at length of the Church as Mystery, People of God, Body of Christ, Temple of the Holy Spirit. But these images seem to refer more to the style than to the substance of ecclesial life. The bishop in the local church possesses a unique and exclusive primacy of ministry in such wise that all other ministry is derivative from his and wholly dependent upon his. He alone is fully priest, prophet and king in imitation of Christ. All others who ex-ercise a ministry are called to assist the bishop and thus share in varying degrees in his prophetic, priestly and governing functions to the extent that he determines he needs their assistance. One gets the impression that, if the diocese were small enough, the bishop could get along nicely without deacons and religious.

In this model of the Church religious, although having charisms proper to themselves, play a role in the Church only as collaborators with the bishop. As chief minister of the Gospel in his diocese the bishop has a special ministry to exercise with respect to religious. This pastoral ministry to religious is highlighted and stressed throughout Part I. The bishop must look upon religious as members of his people and minister to them as well. Although he is precluded from intruding into the internal affairs of the religious com-munities in his diocese, nevertheless he is said to bear the responsibility within his church of promoting, safeguarding and regulating the charisms of religious communities.

This is probably the most troubling aspect of *MR* from the point of view of religious. There is little difficulty in accepting the relationship of religious in-stitutes to the hierarchy as described in *Lumen gentium*, 43. There it is said that "the authority of the Church, led by the Holy Spirit, has taken care to interpret the evangelical counsels, to moderate their practice and to establish stable ways of living them." That this is done by the bishops in council, acting in a fully collegial manner, or by the first bishop, the Pope as universal pastor, presents no serious theological or practical difficulty. But to attribute this function to each bishop in his diocese without a great deal of qualification occasions more than a little concern.

What seems to have happened in the composition of the text of MR is that it inadvertantly confuses the relationship of the bishop to diocesan institutes erected by him or by a predecessor with the considerably different relationship to pontifical institutes, which have an interdiocesan, commonly international function in the Church. What appears as confused in the theoretical presentation becomes far less disturbing in its practical applications. Nevertheless, in the case in point this unnuanced assertion of the responsibility of each individual bishop to exercise pastoral ministry toward the religious in his diocese by "caring for the religious charisms, promoting and safeguarding religious life" (no. 9), could be viewed by some as a mandate to supervise the observance of the counsels and of the rules and the style of community life itself.

Perhaps the most unusual feature of this introductory or systematic part of MR is a quite novel and prolonged analogy between the role of the bishop in his church and that of a religious superior in his or her community (no. 13). The latter is almost quasi-episcopal. Just as the bishop posseses and exercises the three-fold function of teaching, sanctifying and governing his people, religious superiors exercise an analogous role in their communities, which, however, is "not to be confused or set on an equal footing with" the episcopal office (no. 13). While one might be able to speak this way of superiors general or even of other major superiors in some cases, few religious would want to make this claim about a local superior. Religious superiors are said to exercise a sanctifying and governing role, and there is probably little difficulty in this; but when they are said to exercise an authoritative teaching function when they interpret the spirit of their communities and are their spiritual directors, the matter becomes quite problematic. Fortunately this appears to have no impact on the dispositive part of MR.

The later paragraphs of Part I speak of cooperation and collaboration in general terms. It is for the good of the Church as a whole. Religious must help the bishop, follow his lead, and be governed in this by him. Bishops should employ religious in the mission of the Church, but only in ways compatible with the differing charisms and character of each institute. One of the best sections of MR is no. 15 on the mission of the Church. Thereafter the concept of mission becomes central.

Part II of MR, the normative or dispositive provisions, is divided into three sections dealing respectively with formation, apostolic action, and coordination between religious and bishops. Formation is used in a somewhat broader sense than is usual in English and comprehends everything that might be considered education of clergy, religious and laity (nos. 24-35). It deals with the initial formation of religious and of the diocesan clergy and with continuing formation throughout their lives; it speaks of centers, schools and programs jointly undertaken by dioceses and religious communities (nos. 29-31). Special attention is given to the founding and development of centers of pastoral planning and research (no. 32), to publications and the other media of social communication (no. 33). The section on formation concludes with a caution and an enhortation. It cautions religious against excessive independence of the local church, contrasting autonomy and independence (no. 34) and it exhorts bishops and superiors to work cooperatively in the diocesan apostolate, cautioning religious to be informed and aware of diocesan regulations (no. 35).

The second section of Part II (nos. 36-51) addresses the apostolic activities of the diocese. The burden of the section, as of the whole document: cooperation, mutual openness, collaboration and mutual respect between the bishop and his clergy and religious communities. It calls for cooperative planning for new, as well as traditional, ministries (nos. 38, 40).

Some specific prescriptive paragraphs can be highlighted. Bishops and religious superiors should cooperatively remedy abuses which have crept in, especially in the liturgy (no. 43); religious are subject to the regulations of the diocese in everything touching public worship and the apostolate (no. 44, which is verbatim from CD no. 34, 4); even if religious are engaged in works of the diocese which are not those of their own communities they must have a substantial community life and observe their own rules (no. 46). Bishops and their clergy should be made aware of the status and the nature of religious communities and their progress in renewal, while religious superiors should be fully informed about the status and planning of apostolic action in the diocese (no. 47). Among themselves religious superiors in the diocese should meet regularly concerning the religious life and cooperation in apostolic works (no. 48). The expanding and changing role of women, especially of religious women, requires encouragement and special cooperation between the diocese and communities of women (nos. 49-50). The section concludes with a caution about and criteria for establishing new religious institutes (no. 51).

The third section of Part II is concerned with the structures of the cooperation, communication, and collaboration called for throughout MR. The bishop should develop close relationships with men and women religious superiors in order to exercise his pastoral ministry toward them effectively. In their turn these superiors should look on the bishop as the shepherd of the diocese and as their own protector (no. 52). For some reason no. 44 is repeated here, now using the statement of ES I, 25, rather than CD, no. 35 (no. 53). It is recommended that there be an episcopal vicar in each diocese for institutes of religious men and women (no. 54), although it is not clear what function such a local ordinary would have, at least with respect to pontifical institutes. The bishop should persuade the diocesan clergy to welcome religious into the diocesan apostolate and to accept an even wider role for them (no. 55). Religious priests should be members of the senate of priests; religious priests, brothers and sisters should be members of the pastoral council (no. 56). The distinction is clarified, which is found in *ES* I, 30, between works which are proper or belong to religious institutes, and works entrusted to them by the bishop (no. 57). In the case of the latter category there should be written agreements between the diocese and the religious institute, securing the right of the bishop to dismiss and of the religious superior to recall any religious in such works (no 58). Associations of religious men and women are said to be very useful at the diocesan level (no. 59).

What is said here implies regular meetings of religious superiors in the diocese with the bishop (and members of his staff), as well as among themselves. This may be somewhat wide of the mark in our country. Presumably the superiors in question are local superiors. This seems to exaggerate or misunderstand the role of local superiors in many communities both of men and of women. *MR* presumes considerable knowledge of and control over the apostolic work of his or her local community, which often is not the case. Indeed, often enough the director of a work, e.g. at school, hospital, social center, retreat center, will be someone other than the local superior. Misidentifying the appropriate religious personnel could easily result in less cooperation and communication than is the goal of the document.

In the case of major superiors — provincials and superiors general — especially in the case of communities which staff apostolic works in several dioceses, prodigious amounts of time can be, and in some cases already are, required in order to participate in the meetings envisaged by *MR*, which certainly go far beyond an occasional courtesy call on the bishop and anticipate that such superiors of all the communities in the diocese would come together either by themselves or with the bishop. Many major superiors have houses in a fairly large number of dioceses, often spread over great distances. At the same time these are precisely the community leaders whom the bishop wants to influence and to count on. They normally control the placement of personnel and the allocation of financial support, as well as the decisions about entering into or withdrawing from various works.

The remainder of the third section of Part II concerns relations between bishops and religious at the national or regional level (nos. 60-65) and even at the international or global level (no. 66).

Mutuae relationes concludes with an exhortation to bishops and religious to work together in a spirit of true commitment to the Church. It correctly notes that no amount of norms or structures can be effective unless they are persuaded interiorly that they can and should cooperate with each other wholeheartedly.

RICHARD A. HILL, S.J., JCD
Berkeley, California

85

CATHOLIC EDUCATION

Canons 793 through 821 on Catholic education in the Code replace the 1917 Code's canons 1372 to 1383 on schools. The material is reordered and somewhat developed, based partially on the Declaration on Christian Education of the Second Vatican Council. The new canons are arranged with three preliminary canons, then a chapter on schools, a chapter on Catholic universities, and a chapter on ecclesiastical universities.

The first two canons repeat the traditional doctrine of the right of parents to educate their children, the right of parents to assistance in this from civil society, and the right of the Church to educate in virtue of its mission.

Canon 795 defines *education*, quoting from Vatican II's Declaration on Christian Education: "True education is directed toward the formation of the human person in view of his final end, and the good of that society to which he belongs . . . children and young people thus should be helped to develop harmoniously their physical, moral and intellectual qualities. They should be trained to acquire gradually a more perfect sense of responsibility . . . and acquire the right use of liberty . . . and be prepared to take their part in the life of society." *Catholic education* is defined as education in accordance with the principles of Catholic doctrine (canon 803, §2) and *Catholic religious education*, whether done in schools or in the mass media, is subject to the authority of the Church (canon 804, §1).

Schools

The prohibition of canon 1374 of the 1917 Code against Catholic children being sent to non-Catholic, neutral, or mixed schools without permission of the ordinary and in accordance with instructions from the Holy See has been removed. In its place, the freedom of parents to choose schools is recognized (canon 797). They should choose schools in which Catholic education is provided, or at least they should provide such Catholic education themselves outside of schools (canon 798).

Canon 803 defines a Catholic school as a school moderated by ecclesiastical authority or a public ecclesiastic juridic person. For a school to use the name "Catholic" in its title, it must be recognized as Catholic by ecclesiastical authority in writing. Catholic religious education, as distinguished from Catholic education, or education in general, is subject to ecclesiastical authority (canon 804 corresponding to canon 1381 of the 1917 Code). The episcopal conference should publish general norms on Catholic religious education. The bishop develops policies and has vigilance over such education. The diocesan bishop also has the right to visit Catholic schools in his territory and to publish general policy regarding such Catholic schools (canon 805).

Finally, the local ordinary has the right to name and approve teachers of religion and, if necessary, to remove or demand that they be removed (canon 806).

Catholic Universities and Ecclesiastical Universities

In the 1917 Code, Catholic universities are described in canons 1376, 1377, 1378, 1379, §2, and canon 1380. These canons have been considerably developed in the new law and in the October, 1981 consultation several additional changes were adopted.

The basic distinction between Catholic universities and ecclesiastical universities is not in the 1917 Code and is new with the revised one. A *Catholic university*, faculty or institute of higher studies is defined as a university dedicated to higher human culture and the full promotion of the human person, and is an exercise of the teaching office of the Church (canon 807).

In Catholic universities, a faculty or institute of theology, or at least a chair of theology should be erected and lectures in Catholic teaching should be held (canon 811). An *Ecclesiastical university*, on the other hand, is a function of the Church's specific office of announcing revealed truth, and is a university or faculty in which sacred disciplines are investigated and scientifically taught to the students. The main canonical difference between Catholic universities and ecclesiastical universities, especially after the October, 1981 consultation, is the degree of subjection to ecclesiastical authority.

The 1917 Code (canon 1376) states that the canonical constitution of Catholic universities or faculties is reserved to the Holy See and the Holy See must also approve their statues. The new Code states the right of the Church to erect and moderate universities, and the role of the episcopal conference in making sure that Catholic universities are aptly distributed in the territory (canon 809). The October consultation recommended that a phrase about the legitimate scientific autonomy be inserted into this canon. In Catholic universities the competent ecclesiastical authority erects the faculty of theology, as we stated above (canon 811), and it is the role of the episcopal conference and the diocesan bishop to have vigilance over the principles of Catholic doctrine in Catholic universities. No Catholic university can bear the name "Catholic" without consent of the competent ecclesiastical authority (canon 808). The original schema demanded concession from the Apostolic See. This was changed at the October, 1981 consultation. It is the ecclesiastical university which, in accordance with the new law, needs erection by the Holy See; its statutes as well as the "Ratio Studiorum" must be approved by the Holy See (canon 816).

For Catholic universities, the competent ecclesiastical authority would presumably be, therefore, the episcopal conference and the diocesan bishops. It should be noted that in the new Code, the statutes of the Catholic universities should determine which authority is competent to hire professors and to remove them in accordance with procedures determined in the statutes. A reference in the earlier schema to the power of the episcopal conference and-diocesan bishop to demand that teachers be removed for reasons of violation of faith and morals was deleted by the October consultation (canon 810). It is only those professors who treat theological disciplines that must have a mandate of a competent ecclesiastical authority (canon 812). The October consultation changed the expression "canonical mission" to "mandate," and removed the requirement that subjects connected with theology also demanded such a mandate.

Finally, the new Code directs the diocesan bishop to be responsible for the pastoral care of the students at a Catholic university, either through the erection of a parish, or at least through the assignment of priests to this work. Moreover, the diocesan bishop should provide, even in non-Catholic universities, a Catholic university center, which can provide aid, especially spiritual, to the young people attending that university (canon 813).

In summary, the competent ecclesiastical authority grants permission for the use of the name "Catholic" in the title of a Catholic university, has vigilance over the principles of Catholic doctrine, is directed to erect a faculty, institute, or chair of theology, and confers a mandate on professors who teach theological disciplines. The competent ecclesiastical authority is presumably the episcopal conference and the local bishop, not the Holy See. The ecclesiastical authority does not have power to hire and fire other professors or interfere in the scientific autonomy of disciplines other than theology, unless of course, the statues of the univerisity were to give such authority.

Matters are quite different with *ecclesiastical universities.* As mentioned above, ecclesiastical universities cannot be erected without the approval of the Holy See and such universities must have their statutes approved by the Holy See (canon 816). Several of the canons regarding Catholic universities also apply to ecclesiastical universities: the statutes of the ecclesiastical university must define the competent authority for naming professors and for seeing to their removal in accordance with procedures defined by the statutes. The vigilance of the episcopal conference and diocesan bishop over the principles of Catholic doctrine in universities applies to the ecclesiastical university as well as the Catholic university. Professors of theological disciplines require a mandate from the competent ecclesiastical authority in the ecclesiastical university and the diocesan bishop is asked to take responsibility for the pastoral care of the students.

Finally, canon 1377 of the 1917 Code regarding academic grades which have canonical effect is repeated in the new law. Such academic degrees cannot be conferred except by universities or faculties erected or approved by the Holy See. The following are some examples of academic degrees which have canonical effect.

Canon 253, states that professors of philosophy, theology and canon law in seminaries must have a doctorate or license in a university or faculty recognized by the Holy See. In the section on procedure, judicial vicars and adjutant judicial vicars (canon 1420, §4), tribunal judges (canon 1421), the promoter of justice and defender of the bond (canon 1435), must all have a doctorate or license in canon law. Advocates must have a doctorate or be otherwise expert in canon law (canon 1483). Bishops, in order to eligible for promotion to the order of bishop, must have a doctorate or license in scripture, theology, or canon law in an institute approved by the Holy See, or at least have equivalent expertise (canon 378, §1, 5°), and the vicars general and episcopal vicars must have a doctorate or license in theology or canon law or at least equivalent expertise (canon 478, §1). Canon 1378 of the 1917 Code permitting doctors to wear a ring and requesting ordinaries to give preference in conferring certain offices and benefices to those who have at least a license has been dropped. Even though equivalent experience to a license or doctorate is not mentioned in the new law, either for seminary professors or for the primary tribunal officers (judges, promoters of justice and defenders of the bond), the law will, in this country, be interpreted widely out of pastoral necessity, in my opinion.

BERTRAM F. GRIFFIN, JCD
Portland, Oregon

THE SACRAMENT OF PENANCE

The new law on the Sacrament of Penance is contained in canons 959-991 and corresponds to canons 870-936 of the 1917 Code. Some simplification has occurred in the new law; the basic changes regard the law on general absolution and universal jurisdiction for confessors.

Regarding the subject of the sacrament, there has been little change. Canon 988 adds the word "gravia" to the obligation to confess one's sins annually. This is not a change, but a clarification as we know. The 1917 Code demanded that Catholics confess their sins annually. The theologians interpret this as an obligation to confess only grave sins; the new law actually spells this out. It should be noted here that in the terminology of the new law sins are not divided into mortal and venial, but rather into grave and venial sins.

The eight canons in the 1917 Code concerning reservation of sins have been omitted.

Canons 961-963 deal with general absolution. General absolution can be given in danger of death, or when there is grave necessity (for example, the number of penitents). In order to receive general absolution, one must be properly disposed and have the intention to confess grave sins individually in due time. This intention is required for valid reception of the sacrament. Finally, it is clearly stated that when a person has received absolution from grave sin by general absolution, he or she is obliged to approach individual confession when the occasion arises and should not again receive general absolution unless a just cause intervenes.

Canon 964 states that the episcopal conference can establish norms for the place of confession provided, however, that the confessional seat have a grill between the penitent and the confessor so that those who wish to use it may do so. The option of face-to-face confession remains.

The major change in the sacrament is the fact of universal jurisdiction (canons 967-968). In summary, the pope, cardinals and bishops, by the law itself, have jurisdiction to hear confessions anywhere in the world. This faculty of bishops, it should be noted, can be restricted by local ordinaries. Moreover, presbyters who have territorial faculties by reason of office or commission, will, by reason of law, have those faculties extended to anywhere in the world. This would include other ordinaries, the canon penitentiaries, pastors and others who take the place of the pastor, superiors of religious institutes or clerical societies of apostolic life of pontifical rite (for their own subjects and residents in their houses). Those who receive territorial faculties by commission include the following.

1. Priests can receive such faculties from their own ordinary where they are incardinated. These priests, by the very fact of receiving such faculties, have by law, faculties extended throughout the world. If the faculties are revoked by their own ordinary, they also lose such universal faculties. If they are outside their own diocese of incardination, and faculties are revoked by another bishop, this revocation only applies to that territory. These faculties are lost by excardination.
2. Priests may receive faculties by commission from the ordinary of the place where they have a domicile. In such cases, the ordinary should inform the ordinary of incardination. The faculties are lost by losing the domicile. If the faculties are revoked, the ordinaries should inform the ordinary of incardination or the religious superior. Nevertheless, when such faculties are given, even by the ordinary of domicile, rather than by the ordinary of incardination, the faculties are immediately extended by law to the universal Church.

Under the new law, habitual faculties to hear confessions must be given in writing (canon 973). As in the 1917 Code, those who have habitual faculties, either by reason of office or by reason of commission, can delegate others to hear confessions, but only "per modum actus." Canon 132 states that habitual faculties are ruled by the same norms as those for delegated power. Canon 137 states that those who have delegated faculties (and faculties to hear confession by commission would be delegated faculties) may further delegate, but only *per modum actus*. The canon also states that those who have ordinary power (and this would include faculties to hear confession by reason of office) can delegate both *per modum actus* and for all cases, unless the law provides otherwise. Canon 969 states that only the local ordinary can grant habitual faculties to a visiting priest to hear confessions. As an interesting corollary, it would seem that if the ordinary were to grant habitual faculties to a priest who is only visiting the diocese or has only a quasi-domicile in that diocese, then the extension of those faculties to the universal Church would not apply.

As a result of this new legislation on universal jurisdiction, the present canon on faculties to hear confession on the high seas has been omitted. It should also be noted that the requirement of special faculties for hearing confessions of religious women is also dropped from the new Code.

Finally, it is important to note that the new Code retains the "Ecclesia supplet" law in canon 144.

The twenty-six canons on indulgences in the 1917 Code have been reduced to six, and canon 997 of the revised Code refers all other legislation regarding the concession and use of indulgences to special laws such as the *Enchiridion Indulgentiarum*.

BERTRAM F. GRIFFIN, JCD
Portland, Oregon

SACRAMENT OF ANOINTING OF THE SICK

These canons, 998-1007, correspond to canons 937-947 of the 1917 Code of Canon Law. Little change has been made. The few changes that have been made can be reduced to four.

1. The title of the sacrament, as we know, has been changed from extreme unction to anointing of the sick. With this change, the title in law is also changed.
2. Now, oil may be blessed by any presbyter during celebration of the sacrament and in case of necessity (canon 999). In the former law, a presbyter needed an indult from the Holy See.
3. Now, oil may be kept personally by every priest for cases of emergency (canon 1003, §3). Under the former law, pastors needed permission of the bishop to retain oils in their home or rectory.
4. The concept of conditional anointing is eliminated. In cases of doubt, regarding the use of reason, the degree of danger of the infirmity, or doubt regarding death, the law states now that the priest may anoint. Under the previous law they were advised to anoint conditionally (canon 1005).

The rest of the law is substantially the same. Only a presbyter or bishop may administer the sacrament and the conditions for reception are the same as in the old law — that the persons to be anointed have reached the age of discretion or have the use of reason, that the person be a baptized member of the faithful, and that the person be dangerously or seriously ill, or in danger because of old age. It should be noted that ICEL is debating how to translate the expression "periculose aegrotantes" which appears both in the ritual and in canon 1005, defining the sacrament. It seems that ICEL is tending toward the expression "seriously" ill rather than "dangerously."

Besides the above mentioned changes, three collateral issues should be discussed.

1. Refusal of the Sacrament. The new law, canon 1007, is substantially the same as canon 942 of the 1917 Code. The word "mortal" sin has been changed to "grave" sin as occurs throughout the new law. Under the 1917 Code, manifest, grave and obstinant sin is a reason for the refusal of the sacrament of anointing. Moreover, the excommunicated (canon 1282) and the interdicted

(canon 1283) were forbidden to receive this sacrament. There was some debate in the October, 1981 meeting about eliminating this restriction, but to no avail. Nevertheless, the new Code does give wide discretion to confessors in remitting penalties, and hence, indirectly permits the administration of the anointing of the sick in all but the most cantankerous of people. Canon 976, for example, states that in danger of death, any priest can absolve from any sin or censure. Canon 1357 states that outside the danger of death, a confessor can remit *latae sententiae* excommunications and interdicts (which have not been declared or reserved to the Holy See) when a penitent finds it difficult to remain in a state of grave sin for the time necessary to have recourse to a competent superior. Even when absolved, however, the penitent, either directly or through the confessor, must have recourse within a month. It should also be noted that this obligation to recur applies also to those absolved in danger of death if they recover, and the censure was declared, imposed or reserved to the Holy See.

2. The second issue is that of communicatio in sacris. The whole discipline, as you know, has been changed by the Second Vatican Council and is contained in canon 844.

The sacraments of penance, Eucharist and anointing of the sick can now be shared in the following circumstances.

Catholics can receive these sacraments from non-Catholic ministers under four conditions:

a. necessity or true spiritual utility
b. no danger of error or indifferentism
c. physical or moral impossibility of receiving the sacraments from a Catholic minister
d. assurance that the sacraments in the non-Catholic church are valid (canon 844, §2).

The Orthodox may receive the sacraments of penance, Eucharist and anointing of the sick from Catholic ministers when they spontaneously ask for the sacraments and are rightly disposed. This privilege can be extended to members of other churches if the Holy See so judges (canon 844, §3).

Other baptized non-Catholics may also receive these sacraments under six conditions:

a. they cannot approach their own ministers
b. they spontaneously request the sacrament
c. they are rightly disposed
d. they manifest Catholic faith regarding these sacraments
e. they are in danger of death
f. or if there is another grave necessity in the judgment of either the diocesan bishop or the episcopal conference (canon 844, §4).

General norms of the above cases can be given by the bishop or episcopal conference, but only after appropriate ecumenical consultation (canon 844 §5).

3. The final collateral issue is the pastoral theological issues which have

emerged in this country, both from the ministry of permanent deacons who have sought permission to celebrate the sacrament of the anointing of the sick, and from parish experiences in common celebration of the sacrament when parents bring infant children to be anointed. On the basis of these experiences, sometimes the question is posed even more theoretically: Is the sacrament of anointing an extension of baptismal healing, or is it specifically an extension of *Pax*, or sacrament of reconciliation, as was traditionally taught? Without solving the theoretical debate, the present law retains the historic restrictions. Only presbyters and bishops can celebrate the sacrament, and in order to receive the sacrament, the person must have reached the age of discretion or have the use of reason. The usual reason given for these restrictions is that the sacrament, like the *Pax*, or reconciliation, grants forgiveness of sins and reconciliation with the Church, if necessary, and hence can only be celebrated by the bishop or his presbyters, who preside over reconciliation. Moreover, the person receiving the sacrament must be of an age when the sacrament of reconciliation could also be received. Other pastoral theologians have been maintaining that the sacrament is separable from the sacrament of reconciliation and can be viewed as an extension of the healing of baptism, that therefore deacons could celebrate the sacrament and, just as infants can be baptized, so they could benefit from this sacrament of healing. The theoretical discussion will still probably continue.

The new Code does have a definition of the anointing of the sick which was not contained in the 1917 Code. Canon 998 states the Church commends the dangerously (or seriously) ill to the suffering and glorified Lord, that He may raise them up and save them. Though the theoretical issue is not resolved and would not be resolved by the law, the pastoral question has been resolved. Only priests can celebrate the sacrament (canon 1003, §1) and the recipient of the sacrament must have attained the use of reason (canon 1004, §1).

BERTRAM F. GRIFFIN, JCD
Portland, Oregon

SACRAMENT OF ORDERS

The new law on the sacrament of orders is contained in canons 1008-1054 and corresponds to canons 948 through 1011 of the present law. Three major changes have occurred:

1. the definition of orders
2. the introduction of the permanent diaconate
3. the simplifying of the law on irregularities and impediments.

Canon 1009, §1 now defines orders as the episcopacy, presbyterate and diaconate. The 1917 Code, which was modified by the Second Vatican Council, as you know, included under the concept of order or ordination, the consecration of bishops and first tonsure, as well as the major orders of presbyterate, diaconate and subdiaconate, and the four minor orders of porter, lector, exorcist and acolyte. Lector and acolyte are now no longer considered orders, but are lay ministries. Porter and exorcist or catechist are left to particular law and local initiatives. Sub-diaconate has been dropped and is equivalent to the lay ministry of acolyte. First tonsure is replaced by the liturgical celebration of candidacy (canon 1034). Strictly speaking, however, one only becomes a cleric by ordination to the diaconate (canon 266, §1).

An interesting comment could be made regarding the shift in popular language. Although the language bishop, presbyter and deacon is contained in the 1917 Code of Canon Law, in popular language the sacrament was viewed as bishop, priest and deacon. Since the Second Vatican Council, the use of the word "presbyter," "presbyterate," "presbyteral council" has become accepted as popular parlance. In canonical language, the word "sacerdos" includes both *episcopus* and *presbyter*. When the law says *presbyter* it means only that; when the law says *sacerdos* it means to include both bishop and presbyter. Hence, the accurate legal description of the sacrament of orders would be the division into priesthood and diaconate (or ordained ministry); and priesthood is divided into the fullness of the priesthood or episcopacy, and the presbyteral order, which is a sharing in the ministerial priesthood of Christ and the episcopal order.

The section on requirements in ordinands and prerequisites for ordination has been somewhat simplified, obviously because of the whole reordering of the concept of orders. With the introduction of the permanent diaconate, the diaconal order is now divided into the transitional deacon (celibate), the celibate permanent deacon, and the married permanent deacon. Ages for the reception of diaconate and presbyterate have been slightly modified. Under the 1917 Code a deacon must be twenty-two years of age; under the new law, a transitional deacon must be twenty-three years of age, a celibate permanent deacon must be twenty-five years of age, and a married permanent deacon, thirty-five years of age. In the 1917 Code the presbyter must be twenty-four years old; in the new law, he must be twenty-five. However, the new law permits the ordinary to dispense one year from these age restrictions.

According to canon 1037, candidates for transitional diaconate or permanent celibate diaconate must make a public acceptance of celibacy prior to reception of the sacrament, unless they are already in perpetual vows in a religious institute. Before receiving diaconate, a candidate must have received the lay ministries of lector and acolyte and exercised them. There must be a six month interval between the reception of acolyte and diaconate. There must also be a six month interval between the order of diaconate and presbyterate for transitional deacons.

The whole concept of *titulus* is omitted in the new law. Hence, there is no longer any reference to ordination under the title of benefice or personal patrimony or pension, or the more usual titles (at least in this country) of service of the diocese or mission, or the religious titles of poverty, common table, or congregation. One is now simply ordained for the service of the particular church.

Finally, the six day retreat prior to orders has been changed to a five day retreat (canon 1039).

Some of the material of the old law is repeated in a new section called "Documents and Scrutiny." The law, however, has been somewhat simplified. Testimonial letters, banns, and other means of coming to a decision regarding fitness for orders, are left to the discretion of the diocesan bishop or major superior. The rector of the seminary or formation house must testify to the orthodoxy, piety, good morals and aptitude for exercising ministry on the part of candidates. It also must be clear that the candidate has appropriate physical and mental health. The exams or canonical scrutinies prior to orders in the old law have now been replaced by a testimonial of completed studies, although, obviously, particular law could still require examination by pastoral boards.

Similarly, there has been little change in the section on the celebration of orders and the minister. Canon 1010 of the revised Code simplifies the rules on the time for celebration. In effect, the sacrament of orders can be celebrated on Sundays, holy days of obligation, or for pastoral reasons, any day of the week. Canon 1011 states that ordinations should be celebrated in the cathedral, but can be celebrated in other churches or oratories of the diocese for pastoral reasons. The institute of dimissorial letters has been somewhat simplified, but the law remains that one should be ordained by one's own proper bishop or have dimissorials. One's proper bishop, however, is now determined by domicile or intention to serve the local church; place of origin is no longer relevant in determining the proper bishop.

The thorny law on irregularities and impediments has been considerably simplified from the 1917 Code, but is still far from simple. As you know, there are no invalidating impediments to the sacrament of orders. The only condition for valid reception is that the candidate be a baptized male (canon 1024). Impediments are either perpetual (which means they cease only by dispensation) or temporary (which means they can cease by dispensation or by cessation of matter). Perpetual impediments are called irregularities. The expression "impediment" is reserved for the simple or temporary impediments. Secondly, irregularities and impediments can prevent the licit reception of orders and the licit exercise of orders already received.

The division of irregularities into irregularity by defect and delict is retained; however, only one irregularity by defect is in the new law, namely the irregularity of insanity. It should be noted, however, that the irregularity of psychic defect rendering one incapable of ministry is now specifically added to the irregularity of insanity in the new law. As in the old law, if insanity or psychic defect emerges after ordination, it acts as a temporary or simple impediment to the exercise of orders, until after professional consultation, the ordinary judges that the person in question is now fit to exercise such orders.

All other irregularities by defect have been dropped from the new law: illegitimacy (bastardy), physical handicap, epilepsy, demonic possession, bigamy, infamy of law, and the irregularity against judges who have passed the death sentence or executioners who have carried out a capital sentence. Irregularity by delict is now limited to five categories:

1. apostasy, heresy or schism
2. attempted marriage while bound by the diriment impediments of ligamen, orders, or public and perpetual vows of chastity, or marriage with a woman bound by ligamen or vows
3. voluntary homicide and the procuring of or cooperation with a successful abortion
4. self-mutiliation and attempted suicide
5. performing a ministry (act of orders) reserved to bishops or presbyters when not so ordained, or when prohibited by a declared or imposed penalty.

The irregularities by delict of voluntary reception of non-Catholic baptism and clerics exercising the forbidden professions of doctor and surgeon if a death follows have also been dropped from the new law.

Three simple impediments remain:

1. marriage (unless destined for the permanent diaconate)
2. having an office forbidden to clerics which demands civil accountability
3. being a neophyte until judged mature by the ordinary.

The former simple impediments of being children of non-Catholic parents, slaves, still subject to military service, and infamy of fact have been dropped.

The bishop can dispense from the following irregularities against the reception of orders (all else are reserved to the Holy See):

1. insanity and psychic disorders (assuming, of course, that the ordinary, after consulting with the professional, judges that the disorder is cured and would no longer render a candidate unfit for ministry)
2. apostasy, heresy and schism, if occult (not public)
3. attempted marriage against the diriment impediments of ligamen, orders or vows, if the delict is not public (ordinarily, one would assume that the attempted marriage would have also terminated)
4. self-mutilation and attempted suicide, unless the facts had been brought to court
5. a deacon or lay person attempting to exercise a ministry (act of orders) reserved to bishops or presbyters, unless this matter had been referred to ecclesiastical court.

The bishop can dispense from all simple impediments against the reception of orders except that of existing marriage.

The bishop can dispense from all irregularities and impediments against the exercise of orders except:

1. those brought to the judicial forum
2. attempted marriage against the diriment impediments of ligament, orders or vows if the delict is public
3. the delicts of voluntary homicide or performing or positive cooperation in a successful abortion, even if the act is not public.

BERTRAM F. GRIFFIN, JCD
Portland, Oregon

DIACONATE

(Especially the Permanent Diaconate)

According to canon 236, formation for the permanent diaconate must be in accordance with the norms of the episcopal conference. Young men should spend three years in a house of formation prior to ordination. Older men, whether married or celibate, should attend a three year course of studies prior to ordination.

It is through ordination to the diaconate that one becomes a cleric and is incardinated in a particular church for whose service he is ordained (canon 266).

Permanent deacons are generally bound by the obligations of clerics.

In general, deacons like other clerics, must accept offices committed them by the ordinary (canon 274), may not leave the diocese for a notable time without presumed permission by the ordinary (canon 283), owe reverence and obedience to the Holy Father and their own ordinary (canon 273), are united by a common bond of fraternity in prayer and must promote the mission of the laity (canon 275), are obliged to a life of holiness, nourished by scripture and the Eucharist, and to be faithful to the office of pastoral ministry. They are encouraged to participate in daily Mass (canon 276). Celibate clerics must be prudent with their association with women in accordance with diocesan norms (canon 277). Clerics may join associations, especially those which promote spiritual growth and community, but not those which conflict with the tions of ministry (canon 278). Clerics are bound to continue their education (canon 279) and common life is encouraged (canon 280).

Clerics are to lead a simple life-style and contribute to the Church or charity what remains after their own decent support (canon 282). Clerics have a right to a sufficient annual vacation (canon 283, §2).

Clerics are forbidden from military service and should use available exemptions (canon 289).

Permanent deacons are exempt from the following obligations (canon 288):

1. They are not bound to the clerical dress determined by the episcopal conference (canon 284).
2. They are not prohibited from holding public office or managing civil property or funds or having secular offices which require financial accountability. They are exempt from the prohibition

against co-signing for financial obligations (canon 285, §§3 and 4).

3. They are exempt from the prohibition against entering business (canon 286).
4. They are not prohibited from taking an active part in political parties, or from leading labor unions (canon 287, §2).
5. Permanent deacons are not required to recite the Divine Office except as defined by the episcopal conference.

The office of deacon is a sacramental order. The sacrament of orders is divided into episcopacy, presbyterate and diaconate (canon 1009, §1).

Deacons are to be ordained by their proper bishop or with dimissorial letters from the proper bishop. A proper bishop is a bishop of domicile or where one intends to exercise one's service to the Church (canons 1015, 1016).

Transitional deacons must be at least twenty-three years old before ordination and must exercise the diaconate at least six months before ordination to the presbyterate. Celibate permanent deacons must be at least twenty-five years of age; married permanent deacons must be at least thirty-five years old and have permission of their wife (canon 1031). Transitional deacons must have completed the fifth of six years of philosophical theological studies before ordination to the diaconate. After completion of their studies, the deacons must exercise pastoral care in the diaconate before promotion to the presbyterate (canon 1032). Deacons must have previously received and exercised the ministries of lector and acolyte and there must be a six month interval between acoylte and diaconate (canon 1035).

All clerics, including deacons, have a right to fitting remuneration and social assistance. Married deacons, however, may be either stipendiary or not. If non-stipendiary, they ought to be supported by their civil profession or their civil pension or retirement. If they are in full-time ministry and have no civil pension they are to be paid a family living wage (canon 281).

Laws on the teaching office of deacons include the following:

Deacons serve the people of God in the ministry of the Word, in communion with the bishop and his presbyters (canon 757).

Deacons have the faculty to preach everywhere, unless restricted by the ordinary. This faculty, of course, is with the presumed consent of the rector of the church (canon 764).

As clerics, even permanent deacons need permission of the ordinary to write articles in magazines which customarily attack the Catholic religion or good morals, and they must obey the statutes of the episcopal conference regarding participation in radio and T.V. programs which treat questions of Catholic doctrine or morals (canon 831).

Regarding their liturgical office:

The bishop, presbyter and deacon (without prejudice to the rights of the pastor) are the ordinary ministers of baptism (canon 861).

The ordinary minister of Holy Communion is the bishop, presbyter or deacon (canon 910). The deacon is required to wear liturgical vestments while celebrating or ministering the Eucharist (canon 929). The deacon is forbidden to recite prayers proper to the priest, especially the Eucharistic prayer, or perform liturgical actions proper to the priest (canon 907).

The minister of Exposition of the Blessed Sacrament and Benediction is a priest or deacon (canon 943).

Clerics, both priests and deacons, are the usual ministers of sacramentals (canon 1168) and deacons can grant blessings expressly permitted by law (canon 1169, §3).

Deacons may be delegated as official witnesses of a marriage by either the ordinary or the pastor of the parish, and may even receive general delegation (canons 1108 and 1111).

BERTRAM F. GRIFFIN, JCD
Portland, Oregon

THE PASTORAL CARE OF MARRIAGE

Canon 1063 directs that pastors are obliged to see that the proper ecclesial community offers assistance in both proximate and remote preparation for marriage. Canon 1064 directs the ordinary to coordinate such assistance using the experience and expertise of the laity.

Strictly speaking, the impedient impediments to marriage are eliminated. However, in eight cases the ordinary's permission is required. Some of these so-called permissions might well be delegated in diocesan faculties to the local pastor.

1. The marriage of transients
2. Marriages forbidden or not acknowledged by civil law (for example, marriages of undocumented aliens who feel frightened about applying for a civil license, or marriages of senior citizens who do not wish the marriage to be recorded by the State)
3. A marriage of someone who has natural obligations to a former spouse or children
4. The marriage of a minor when parents are unaware or reasonably unwilling
5. Marriage by proxy
6. Marriage of someone who has been excommunicated or interdicted
7. The marriage of notorious ex-Catholics
8. Ecumenical or mixed marriages.

Although ecumenical or mixed marriages are now no longer forbidden, permission of the ordinary is required. The promise on the part of the Catholic party to raise the children Catholic, if possible, is maintained not only for marriages with the impediment of disparity of cult, but with mixed marriages and with marriages of a Catholic and a notorious ex-Catholic.

There are twelve diriment impediments in the new Code:

Canon 1083 — The impediment of age—14 for girls and 16 for boys; the episcopal conference can recommend a higher age for liceity

Canon 1084 — Impotence

Canon 1085 — Previous bond

Canon 1086 — Disparity of cult

Canon 1087 — Sacred Orders (despite earlier proposals, this impediment has been retained even for married deacons who are widowed and wish to remarry)

Canon 1088 — Public vows in a religious institute

Canon 1089 — Kidnap

Canon 1090 — Murder of spouse

Canon 1091 — Consanguinity in the direct line and to the fourth degree collateral line. (It should be noted that the Germanic method of computing relationship has been adopted by the new Code. Under the Roman system and the 1917 Code, collateral degree of relationship is computed by counting the longest line *dempto stirpe*. Under the new law, fourth degree collateral line refers to first cousins, but may also include the relationship of uncle and grand niece.)

Canon 1092 — Affinity in the direct line

Canon 1093 — Public decency, in the first degree of the direct line

Canon 1094 — Adoption in the direct line and the second degree collateral line (adopted brother and sister).

The ordinary and the pastor have general authority to witness marriages within their respective territory (canon 1108). Both can give general delegation to priests and deacons to assist at marriages within their territory.

General delegation must be given in writing (canon 1111, §2).

Personal pastors, by reason of their office, are limited to performing marriages within their territory, where at least one of the parties is a member of their personal parish (canon 1110). Hence, if a personal parish were set up for a university, the pastor would not have authority, even validly, to marry a young couple, unless one of the persons were a student at the university or a member of the faculty or staff. In order to avoid such problems, it would seem wise for the ordinary to grant general delegation for the entire diocese parish priests assigned to personal parishes. It might also be appropriate in many dioceses to extend the pastor's general delegation throughout the diocese by general delegation from the ordinary.

The marriage should be celebrated in the proper parish of either party, or even in a parish where one of the parties may have a month residence, or in the case of transients, in the parish where they are presently residing. Marriages need no longer be celebrated by preference in the parish of the bride. With the permission of the ordinary or the proper pastor, marriages can be celebrated elsewhere (canon 1115). But the reference to domicile or quasi-domicile does not necessarily imply that the territorial parish is given preference since personal parishes also are territorial, but limited to members of a particular language, rite, ethnic origin, etc. in a given territory.

Marriages ordinarily should take place in the parish church. The pastor can permit a marriage to take place in another church or oratory within his territory. Outdoor marriages require the permission of the ordinary. An interesting note is that marriages between a Catholic and a non-baptized person can be celebrated in either a church or any other appropriate place and no permission is required (canon 1118).

BERTRAM F. GRIFFIN, JCD
Portland, Oregon

SACRED PLACES AND TIMES

One of the most popular and most talked about activities in our country today is dieting. The ads are everywhere urging people to take advantage of this or that program. Practically every issue of feature magazines contains a new weight control program. The dieter is to get rid of unnecessary and unsightly fat while toning the muscles to look better.

It would seem the second part of Book III of the 1917 Code went on a very successful weight reduction program. "Sacred Times and Places" has changed quite a bit. From 100 canons it is now only 48. Instead of 11 subheadings there are now 9. The introductory section on sacred places increased to 9 from 7, while the introductory section on sacred times decreased from 4 to 2. Churches and cemeteries lost the most: churches went from 26 to 9 and cemeteries from 38 canons to 4. It must be admitted that there is a new section in Book IV named Certain Acts of Divine Cult which contains 9 canons on ecclesiastical burial (1176-1185) which were in the section on cemeteries before. However, that is still a significant reduction. A section of 5 canons has been added for shrines.

More important than the change in numbers has been the change in tone of the norms. In the 1917 Code cc. 1160 and 1206 are almost beligerent in their tone stating the position of the Church's power vis-à-vis the state. In the 1983 Code this is more subdued in canon 1213 and not mentioned in 1240. The right of asylum in canon 1179 of the 1917 Code is missing from the revised law. Bells are to be heard and not read about. Violation of a church is treated as a violation of any holy place.

The norms which have survived are many times slimmed down themselves. Canon 1223 simplifies the 1917 Code's canon 1188 (oratories), 1235 simplifies the old canon 1197 (altars); the same with 1236 and old canon 1198, and 1241 for the 1917 Code canon 1208 (cemeteries). A casual perusal will give other examples. The law is trying to be broad enough by eschewing specificity. It is almost as if the Church has matured in its ability to read and understand the law. When the word "ordinary" is used, the law seldom sees the need to mention religious (contrast 1206 with 1917 Code canon 1155, 1207 with old canon 1156). The canons on oratories correspond to the notion of a semi-public oratory in the 1917 Code. "Private chapel" is the new term for private or domestic oratories.

The revised law has plenty of new blood infused from trends in the Church today.

Canon 1243 gives to particular law the task of regulating cemeteries.

The prudence of the diocesan bishop is left to decide the uses for a church returned to a profane use (1222). Canon 1220 will allow liturgical norms to maintain a fitting dignity in sacred celebrations; canon 1237, §1 also gives liturgical norms responsibility for determining whether a movable altar needs a dedication.

Canon 1215, §2 requires consultation with the council of presbyters before building a new church. Canon 1224, §1 insists the ordinary himself or through another (*per alium*) visit the site of a new oratory before he allows it to be built. In the 1917 Code, canon 1192, §2 insists the visit be made by the ordinary or "alium ecclesiasticum virum."

The episcopal conference is mentioned in canons 1246 (reducing days of precept), 1251 (food to be avoided on days of abstinence), and 1253 (other forms of penance).

Many have thought of *Poenitemini* as being one of the classic models of legislation. Its footprints are to be found in this revised Code. Canon 1245 giving pastors the power to dispense is from canon 1245 of the 1917 Code, but largely is from *Poenitemini* VII. Canon 1252 is from *Poenitemini* IV and canon 1253 quotes *Poenitemini* VI which is taken from the Pastoral Office of Bishops 38, 4. The quotations from *Poenitemini* as well as the addition of canon 1249 give some value to the section on penance. No longer is the law merely concerned with ages, days and proscriptions, but now it gives the reasons for the penance thus opening a wide range of possibilities for the individual.

In perusing the laws, one can see a practical solution to the problem for pastors of back-to-back days of precept. When the bishops fail to act, the individual pastor may. If a parish or important local celebration is to occur on a Friday of Lent, the penitential day can be commuted. The bishop has the authority to dispense from most of these laws under canon 87.

In summation this section of the revised law appears to be a step forward. It has been trimmed and refined. Greater discretion is left to local authorities and more recognition given to liturgical norms.

ROYCE R. THOMAS, JCL
Little Rock, Arkansas

ECCLESIASTICAL SANCTIONS

The entire maze of canonical penalties has been considerably simplified in the new law. The canonical penalties now remaining are excommunication, interdict from the sacraments, and suspension. Such penalties as infamy and local interdict have been dropped.

Excommunication entails basically three effects. A person excommunicated cannot act as a liturgical minister, cannot celebrate or receive the sacraments or sacramentals, and cannot hold ecclesiastical offices or ministries (canon 1331). In this country only *Latae sententiae* penalties will have a significance. However, in the rare case that an excommunication were declared or imposed, either by ecclesiastical trial or administrative process, additional effects accrue: the person is to be removed or liturgical action should cease if he attempts to act as a liturgical minister. All acts of office are invalid. Persons who are excommunicated cannot enjoy ecclesiastical privileges or validly obtain a dignity or ecclesiastical office, and lose all stipends, salaries and ecclesiastical pensions.

Personal interdict against liturgical participation (canon 1332) means that the person so interdicted cannot act as a liturgical minister or celebrate or receive sacraments or sacramentals. Obviously the main difference between interdict and excommunication is the issue of ecclesiastical office or ministry.

Again, in this country interdict will rarely, if ever, be declared or imposed by an ecclesiastical trial or administrative process. However, if this were to occur, then such a person would have to be removed or the liturgical action cease if he attempted to act as a liturgical minister.

There are now only seven automatic or *latae sententiae* excommunications. Five of these are reserved to the Apostolic See: desecration of the Blessed Sacrament (canon 1367), laying violent hands on the pope (canon 1370, §1), absolving an accomplice (canon 1378, §1), a bishop consecrating another bishop without mandate (both are excommunicated—canon 1382), and direct violation of the seal of confession (canon 1388, §1). The two remaining automatic excommunications are for apostasy, heresy or schism (canon 1364, §1), and for a successful abortion (canon 1398).

There are five automatic liturgical interdicts: (1) laying violent hands on a bishop (canon 1370, §2); (2) simulating the Eucharist (canon 1378, §2); (3) attempting to give invalid absolution (canon 1378, §2); (4) false denunciation of a confessor (canon 1390, §1); and (5) a religious who is not a cleric attempting marriage (canon 1394, §2).

In danger of death, any priest can absolve from any censure. Ordinarily, a confessor needs special faculties even for absolving from undeclared and non-reserved censures.

If a cleric commits a delict subject to automatic excommunication, he is by the very nature of the penalty of excommunication, suspended. If he commits one of the delicts punishable by automatic liturgical interdict, he is also thereby suspended.

In addition, there are two further automatic suspensions in the new law: attempted marriage (canon 1394, §1) and receiving orders from someone other than one's own proper bishop without dimissorial letters (canon 1383). It should be noted that a bishop conferring such order is suspended for one year from conferring of additional orders.

Suspension refers only to clerics and includes all or some acts of the power of orders, all or some acts of the power of jurisdiction or Church government, and the exercise of all or some rights or functions belonging to an office. A suspension does not affect the right to remain in the rectory if such right is attached to the office; it does not affect the right to a decent living and support from the Church; if the penalty is *latae sententiae* it does not affect the right to continue administering an office.

All censures must be imposed by due process, either through ecclesiastical trial or by administrative process. Even if a censure is imposed by an administrative decree, a clear process must be used. The person must be warned and given time for repentence before the process may proceed and this is required for validity (canon 1347, §1). The person must be informed of accusations and proofs and has the right to defend him or herself (canon 1720). Two assessors must be used to weigh the arguments and proofs. Even an administrative decree cannot impose a perpetual penalty (canon 1342, §2) nor can a judge (canon 1349).

Finally, administrative acts, even impositions of penalties, can be referred to the hierarchical superior if there is question of the legitimacy of the penalty, the violation of procedural norms, or the penalty is imposed because of facts that are not true.

This section on expiatory penalties (canon 1336-1338) only applies to clerics and religious and is probably inoperative in this country, at least as penal law, except for the possible penalty of dismissal from the clerical state for grave scandal or for grave crimes. Even if a cleric is required to spend some time in a house of prayer or a "guest house", this is ordinarily not considered penal, but an attempt to rehabilitate someone from alcohol or chemical dependency.

Similarly, the section on penances and penal remedies (canon 1339-1340) is probably irrelevant for the American Church, other than the note that public penances can never be imposed for non-public transgressions.

BERTRAM F. GRIFFIN, JCD
Portland, Oregon

"INTERNAL FORUM SOLUTION"

I. Scope of Concern

The pastoral care of those involved in irregular unions, i.e., those who have divorced and remarried civilly, is sometimes considered under the heading of the "internal forum solution," or the moral and canonical aspects of their reconciliation to the community by means of admission to the sacraments of penance and Eucharist.

II. Remarks

A. This is primarily a moral matter involving the discernment of the state of grace, of living in a proximate occasion of sin, good conscience, and the criteria of worthiness for the reception of Holy Communion. The processes of counseling and judgment take place in the forum of conscience.

B. An overview of the recent history of the question in the U.S.
1. 1930's and 1940's: only alternative to separation of the spouses was the "brother-sister" relationship
2. 1940's: innovation and spread of the "good faith" solution
3. 1972: Baton Rouge inaugurated a systematic program of use of internal forum; warning from Holy Office not to innovate, matter under study
4. 1973: response from Cardinal Seper; NCCB requested clarification
5. 1975: "clarification" from Archbishop Hamer
6. 1976-78: NCCB attempts to formulate guidelines
7. 1978: Propositions from the International Theological Commission
8. 1981: John-Paul II, Apostolic Exhortation on the Family.

C. Before one resorts to an internal forum solution there is a presumption that the ordinary means of reconciliation in the external forum have been exhausted; i.e., the possibilities of declaration of nullity or dissolution of the previous marriage have been investigated and found not to exist or to be morally impossible.

D. Canonical issues
1. The prohibition of a second marriage until the first is declared null (1917 Code, c. 1069, §2 is repeated in c. 1085, §2) is positive

ecclesiastical law and can yield to the radical right to marry (reaffirmed in *Gaudium et spes*, no. 26).

2. It is possible that the second union may be valid by means of extraordinary form (1917 Code, c. 1098; 1983 Code, c. 1116), if the first union was in fact invalid.

3. The penalty of legal infamy (1917 Code, c. 2356), which was probably rarely incurred and did not have to be observed in the external forum, is not maintained in the new Code. (It was not a bar to the Eucharist unless it was public: 1917 Code, c. 855.)

4. Canon 912 asserts the right of the baptized to the Eucharist if not prohibited by law; c. 915 bars from Communion only those who gravely and publicly commit crime and presevere in their contumacy; c. 916 states that those "conscious of grave sin" are not to communicate.

5. Decree 124 of III Council of Baltimore — the excommunication was rarely incurred because any diminution of imputability excused — was rescinded by the NCCB in May, 1977.

E. Recent authors distinguish the application of the internal forum solution to two different situations:

1. "Conflict" — when there is a well-grounded judgment that the first marriage was null, but that fact cannot be established, e.g., for want of witnesses, evidence, or because of inadequacy of local tribunal, case overload, etc.

2. "Hardship" — when there is no solid evidence that the first union was invalid, and thus it is presumed to have been valid.

F. Criteria for making the moral judgment of reception of sacraments:

1. First marriage irretrievably broken, reconciliation impossible

2. Repentance for any fault for breakdown of first union

3. Willingness to discharge responsibilities for former wife or husband and children

4. Present union appears stable and enduring, obligations of love, fidelity, care of children appropriately assumed

5. Every effort made to minimize scandal; indissolubility of marriage not compromised

6. Desire to live and witness to the faith in the church community.

G. Since this pastoral accommodation is a matter of the internal forum, essentially a matter of conscience, it is very questionable whether any public record or documentation of it should be made anywhere.

III. BIBLIOGRAPHY
(abbreviated; in chronological order)

Peters, Beemer, Van der Poel, "Cohabitation . . .," *Homiletic and Pastoral Review*, 1966.

Haring, Kosnik, Reich, Farley, et al, *The Jurist*, 1970.

Bassett, "Divorce & Remarriage," *American Ecclesiastical Review*, 1970.

McCormick, *Theological Studies*, 1971, 1972, 1975; *C.L.S.A. Proceedings*, 1975.

Tracy, *Catholic Mind*, 1972.

CTSA Committee Report, *Proceedings*, 1972.

Lehmann, "Indissolubility . . .," *Communio*, 1972.

Cong. Doct. Fidei, letters: Seper, 4-11-73; Hamer, 3-21-75.

Curran, *American Ecclesiastical Review*, 1973; C.L.S.A. Proceedings, 1974.

Ryan, *Furrow*, 1973.

International Theological Commission, "Propositions," 1978.

Green, *Chicago Studies*, 1979.

Provost, *The Jurist*, 1980.

Urrutia, *The Jurist*, 1980.

John-Paul II, *Familiaris Consortio*, 1981.

JAMES A. CORIDEN, JCD
Washington, D.C.

"SACRAE DISCIPLINAE LEGES"

On January 25, 1983 Pope John Paul II promulgated the revised Code of Canon Law with the Apostolic Constitution Sacrae Disciplinae Leges. *The following is a translation of the Constitution, provided by NC News Service.*

To our venerable brothers, cardinals, archbishops, bishops, priests, deacons and the other members of the people of God, John Paul, bishop, servant of God for perpetual memory.

Over the course of the centuries, the Catholic Church has regularly reformed and renewed the laws of canonical discipline so that, in constant fidelity to her divine founder, these should adapt themselves well to the saving mission confided to her. Moved by this same purpose and finally bringing to fulfillment the expectation of the whole Catholic world, I today, January 25, 1983, dispose publication of the Code of Canon Law after revision of it. In doing this, my thought returns to the same date of the year 1959, when my predecessor John XXIII announced for the first time his decision to reform the current Code of Canon Law, which had been solemnly promulgated on the solemnity of Pentecost of the year 1917.

The decision to reform the Code was taken together with two other decisions of which that same pontiff spoke on that same day: the intention to celebrate the synod of the the Diocese of Rome and to convoke an ecumenical council. While the former has no strict relevance to reform of the Code, the other, concerning the Council, is of the highest importance to our discourse and is closely linked with it.

If we ask why John XXIII had become aware of the need to reform the current Code, the answer may perhaps be found in the Code itself, promulgated in 1917. A different answer, however, exists and is the decisive one: namely, that reform of the Code of Canon Law was seen to be clearly willed and requested by the same Council, which had given greatest attention to the Church.

As is obvious, when the first announcement of revision of the Code was made, the Council was still in the future. In addition, the acts of its magisterium, namely its doctrine on the Church, were to be set down in the years 1962-1965. Nonetheless, no one can fail to see how John XXIII's intuition was most exact, and it must rightly be said that his decision provided in advance for the good of the Church.

Therefore, the new Code, published today, necessarily recalls the Council's preceding work. Even though it was preannounced together with the Council sessions, it nevertheless chronologically followed them, since the work needed for preparing the new revised Code necessarily had to be based on the Council and thus could not begin until after its conclusion.

Turning my thoughts now to the beginning of that long course, to that January 25, 1959, and to the person of John XXIII himself, promoter of revision of the Code, I must acknowledge that this Code has arisen from a single intention, that of restoring Christian living. All the work of the Council actually drew its norms and its orientation from such an intention.

If we now go on to consider the nature of the labors which have led up to this promulgation of the Code, as well as the manner in which they were conducted, especially during the pontificates of Paul VI and John Paul I, then down to our own days, it is absolutely necessary to point out with all clarity that such labors were brought to conclusion in a markedly collegial spirit. This not only refers to the drafting of the material of the work but also touches on the very substance of the laws drafted.

Now, this note of collegiality characterizes and distinguishes the process giving rise to the present Code; it likewise corresponds perfectly to the magisterium and to the content of the Second Vatican Council. The Code, therefore, not only through its contents, but also through its earliest beginning, demonstrates the spirit of this Council, in whose documents the universal Church, "the sacrament of salvation" (cf. "Dogmatic Constitution on the Church," nn. 1, 9, 48), is presented as the people of God, its hierarchical constitution is seen as founded on the college of bishops jointly with its head.

It was for this reason, therefore, that the bishops and bishops' conferences were invited to collaborate in preparing the new Code, so that, over such a long course, with a method as collegial as possible, the juridical formulas would little by little come to light which would then be for the use of the whole Church. Experts, then, took part in all stages of the labors, that is to say, men specialized in theological doctrine, history, and above all canon law. They were chosen from all parts of the world.

To each of them I desire today to manifest my sentiments of deepest gratitude.

There come before my eyes first of all the figures of deceased cardinals who presided over the preparatory commission: Cardinal Pietro Ciriaci, who began the work, and Cardinal Pericle Felici, who guided the course of the labors almost to their end. Then I think of the secretaries of the same commission: Msgr. Giacomo Violardo, later cardinal, and Father Raimondo Bidagor of the Society of Jesus. Both of these poured out the treasures of their learning and wisdom in this task. Together with them I recall the cardinals, archbishops, bishops and all who were members of that commission, as well as consultors of the individual study groups involved over these years in that difficult task. God has in the meantime called them to their eternal rewards. My prayer rises to God for the souls of all.

I am also pleased to recall the living, beginning with the present propresident of the commission, our venerable brother, Archbishop Rosalio Castillo Lara. He has worked for many years in this undertaking bearing so much responsibility. I go on now to our beloved son, Msgr. William Onclin. His assiduousness and diligence have greatly contributed to the happy conclusions of the work. I would then mention all those others who have given their valued contribution to working out and completing a task so weighty and complex, and have done so as cardinal members, as officials, consultors and collaborators in the various study groups and other offices.

Therefore, as I promulgate this Code today, I am fully aware that this act is an expression of the pontifical authority, and therefore takes on a "primatial" nature; but I am equally well aware that, in its objective content, this Code respects the collegial concern for the Church of all my brothers in the episcopate. Indeed, through a certain analogy with the Council, it must be considered as the fruit of a collegial collaboration to bring together all energies of specialized persons and institutions spread throughout the Church.

A second question now arises about the very nature of the Code of Canon Law. In order to answer this question well, it is necessary to recall the distant heritage of law contained in the books of the Old and New Testaments, from which, as from its first spring, the whole juridical legislation of the Church derives.

Christ the Lord did not in fact will to destroy the very rich heritage of the law and the prophets which had been forming over the course of the history and experience of the people of God in the Old Testament. On the contrary, he gave fulfillment to it (cf. Mt. 5:17). Thus, in a new and more lofty way, it became part of the inheritance of the New Testament. Therefore, although when expounding the paschal mystery, St. Paul teaches that justification is not obtained through the works of the law but through faith (cf. Rom. 3:28; Gal. 2:16), he does not thereby exclude the obligatory force of the Decalogue (cf. Rom. 13:28; Gal. 5:13-25 and 6:2), nor does he deny the importance of discipline in the Church of God (cf. 1 Cor. chapters 5 and 6). The writings of the New Testament, therefore, allow us to understand the importance of discipline even better and to understand better how discipline is more closely connected with the salvific character of the Gospel message itself.

Since this is so, it seems clear enough that the Code in no way has as its scope to substitute for faith, grace, charisms, and especially charity in the life of the Church or the faithful. On the contrary, its end is rather to create such order in ecclesial society that, assigning primacy to love, grace and charisms, it at the same time renders more active their organic development in the life both of the ecclesial society and of the individuals belonging to it.

Inasmuch as it is the Church's prime legislative document, based on the juridical and legislative heritage of revelation and tradition, the Code must be regarded as the necessary instrument whereby due order is preserved in both individual and social life and in the Church's activity. Therefore, besides containing the fundamental elements of the hierarchical and organic structure of the Church, laid down by her divine founder or founded on apostolic or at any rate most ancient tradition, and besides outstanding norms concerning the carrying out of the task mandated to the Church herself, the Code must also define a certain number of rules and norms of action.

The instrument which the Code is fully suits the Church's nature, for the Church is presented, especially through the magisterium of the Second Vatican Council, with her universal scope, and especially through the Council's ecclesiological teaching. In a certain sense, indeed, this new Code may be considered in a certain way as a great effort to transfer that same ecclesiological or conciliar doctrine into canonical language. And, if it is impossible for the image of the Church described by the Council's teaching to be perfectly converted into canonical language, the Code nonetheless must always be referred to in that same image, as the primary pattern whose outline the Code ought to express as well as it can by its own nature.

From this derive a number of fundamental norms by which the whole of the new Code is ruled, of course within the limits proper to it, as well as the limits of the very language befitting the material.

It may rather be rightly affirmed that from this comes that note whereby the Code is regarded as a complement to the magisterium expounded by the Second Vatican Council, particularly as regards the two constitutions (on the Church), the dogmatic and the pastoral.

It follows that the fundamental basis for the "novelty" which, while never departing from the Church's legislative tradition, is found in the Second Vatican Council, especially in what concerns its ecclesiological teaching, is also the basis for the "novelty" in the new Code.

The following elements are most especially to be noted among those expressing a true and genuine image of the Church: the doctrine whereby the Church is proposed as the people of God (cf. "Lumen Gentium," n. 2) and the hierarchical authority is propounded as service (ibid., n. 3). In addition, the doctrine which shows the Church to be a "communion" and from that lays down the mutual relationships which ought to exist between the particular and universal Church and between collegiality and primacy. Likewise the doctrine whereby all members of the people of God, each in the manner proper to him, share in Christ's threefold office of priest, prophet and king. To this doctrine is also connected that regarding the duties and rights of the Christian faithful, particularly the laity. Then there is the effort which the Church has to make for ecumenism.

If, therefore, the Second Vatican Council brought out old and new from the treasury of tradition, and if its novelty is also contained in these other forms, it is manifest that the Code, too, contains that note of fidelity in newness and newness in fidelity, and that it conforms to this as regards its own material and its particular manner of expression.

The new Code of Canon Law is being published precisely when the bishops of the whole world are not only asking for it to be promulgated, but are also insistently and vehemently demanding it.

Indeed, the Code of Canon Law is extremely necessary for the Church. Since it is established for the sake of the manner of her social and visible framework, the Church needs it for her hierarchical and organic structure to be visible; so that exercise of the offices and tasks divinely entrusted to her, especially her sacred power and administration of the sacraments, should be rightly ordered; so that mutual relations of the Christian faithful may be carried out according to justice based on charity, with the rights of all being safeguarded and defined; so that we may then prepare and perform our common tasks, and that these, undertaken to live a Christian life more perfectly, may be fortified by means of the canonical laws.

Thus canonical laws require to be observed by their very nature. Hence it is of the greatest importance that the norms shall be carefully expounded on the basis of solid juridical, canonical, and theological foundations.

In consideration of all these things it is naturally to be desired that this new canonical legislation will be an effective instrument which the Church herself may use to perfect herself in accordance with the Second Vatican Council, so that she may make herself ever more equal to her salvific task in this world.

We are pleased to commit these considerations of ours to all in a trusting spirit as we promulgate this principal body of ecclesiastical legislation for the Latin Church.

May God ensure that joy and peace with justice and obedience shall commend this Code, and that what is commanded by the head may be obeyed by the body.

Therefore, relying on devine grace, borne up by the authority of the blessed apostles Peter and Paul, assenting to the certain knowledge and the prayers of the bishops of the whole world who collaborated with us in collegial affection, we, by the supreme authority which we exert, and which is to hold good in the future by virtue of this our Constitution, promulgate the present Code such as it has been digested and inspected; we command that it shall have force henceforth for the universal Latin Church and we give it to be guarded by the ward and vigilance of all those to whom it applies. In order, however, that all may more accurately convey these prescripts rightly and may be able to get to know them clearly before they enter into effect, we decree and command that they shall be endowed with obligatory force from the first day of Advent of the year 1983, all ordinances, constitutions, and privileges, even those worthy of special and individual mention, and customs notwithstanding.

We therefore exhort all our beloved children to observe the precepts laid down with sincere mind and ready will, borne up by hope, that a fervent discipline may burgeon again in the Church and that thereby salvation of souls will be made always easier, under the protection of the most Blessed Virgin Mary, Mother of the Church.

Given at Rome, the 25th day of January of the year 1983, in the Vatican Palace, in the fifth year of our pontificate.

JOANNES PAULUS PP II.